Zero's Blooming Excursion

Zero's Blooming Excursion

Jared Schickling

BlazeVOX [books]

Buffalo, New York

Zero's Blooming Excursion by Jared Schickling

Printed in the United States of America

Book design by Geoffrey Gatza
Cover art, "untitled," by Alec Maslowski

First Edition
ISBN: 978-1-60964-001-9
Library of Congress Control Number 2010906696

BlazeVOX [books]
303 Bedford Ave
Buffalo, NY 14216

Editor@blazevox.org

publisher of weird little books

BlazeVOX [books]

blazevox.org

2   4   6   8   0   9   7   5   3   1

B   X

Acknowledgments

Portions of this poem were first published in *ditch, the poetry that matters, Mayday Magazine,* and *H_NGM_N.* Thank you, John C. Goodman, David Bowen and Okla Elliott, and Nate Pritts. Thank you, for reading, assistance, guidance, friendship, without which this work would not have been possible, Dan Beachy-Quick, Sasha Steensen, Matthew Cooperman, Jerrod Bohn, Sunshine Dempsey, Crane Giamo, Kelley Irmen, Rico Moore, Susie Tepper, Brad Vogler, Jeffrey Snodgrass. Thank you, Chuck Richardson, most brilliant reader, thinker, storyteller, honest and ethical critic and friend I could hope for. Thank you, Geoffrey Gatza and BlazeVOX, for the continued support of this work, and that of others, for supporting a certain *kind* of work. Thank you, especially, Mollie, my wife, without whom I don't do anything. Thank you, Pat Lowther, for the education, friendship, the enigma some of us live with.

Zero's Blooming Excursion

Zero's Blooming Excursion

he loved to address having seen him
his new man years which is invisible
covered, redacted i fear not what man
but found can do unto me

Old Glory

i   .i

Fable

note from his Text

FABLE?

Patrick Lowther.

The dreadful and curious thing is that men, despoiled and having nothing, must long most for that which they have not and so, out of the intensity of their emptiness imagining they are full, deceive themselves and all the despoiled of the world into their sorry beliefs. It is the spirit that existing nowhere in them is forced into their dreams. The ███████ they, the seed, instead of growing, look black at the world and damning its perfections praise a zero in themselves. Each shrinks from an imagination that severs him from the rest.

"One within a silence where none can speak
"The war that matters is the war against the ███████ some
rested their heads upon ████████ as on a pillow for weariness the rest
tossed and reeled and danced seemed
To do alone the work no one can do alone"

"There is no longer any credible way
interior, pastoral refuge
"If reality were not absolute
from the ████████ of culture
████████████ would of course be impossible"

OLD GLORY

1 there on the filthy waters [1]

---

[1] There was here and there a little knot, and a few stragglers a few yards higher up; but they were so few as not to disturb the simplicity, unity, and life of that one busy highway.

♂

MERGER OF THE PINEAL GLANDS

HURON—   herons' nest

                                        ABOUT THE TIME O THE FIRST

            way o the *peer* EARS QUOI FIRST   HARVESTS'
wilder roach, way beneath the bottle's   port   E
Would be bogged down in helping WALLEYE   R
CONSIDERED help *caked*   A MARKER OF CLEAR WATER
SILURIAN   WHERE LAMPREY WERE BEING——POISONING

            JUVENILE   STAGE

sand jammed GRAPHIC   aurora DEPICTING A SUM——   T = (1/n)(2L/√(gd))
sands arched along   PROPAGATING WAVES TRAVELING
the red OPPOSITE   DIRECT
      ions purple and blue

            GLACIERS   LEE
                                        FLAG modified for arbitrary depth:
smelt—   helping or   T = 2√(2πL/(gTANh(πh/L)))
            clap—   not helping *lays* less
      yolk's LICKED leaching   COSMOGONIC *eggs*
GULLS near its anus   whitish   —at the beach

            the rod too'd rust—wave

come down ABOUT THE TIME OF THE FIRST HARVESTS'
Carousel, scaffolding, kid, grass what was "olcott" nightlife some LODGES
deepened IN THE BAY O AN OCEAN
BUT THE LAND REBOUNDING   RELEASED released—

                        "high water level
                        undermining break
                  water—the people pissed

                  their *piers* BUT THE TILT AMPLIFIES THIS
            EFFECTS where arrowheads' trapped CAUSING LOSS TO PROPERTY
OWNERS' Other implement
            steadies—

"in somerset coalstack yr barges by truck

in stock,
backyards'

POTENTIAL, EPIPELAGIC t + 2m if

amortized BENZAPYRENE O(log n)   LEAD MIREX MERCURY'S
banks'   ARA—pronounced   CARBON
TETRA   CHLORID   "doych" *sic* MITE   GERM'S OLDe fart niagaras be
Σ carried some—WEE   B E   E E wonder there's amish—?

"natural seiche rhythm"
GRAPHIC DEPICTING A SUM

DANCED catalyzed *cocoon*   11 miNUTES'   NEWT'S
drills FILAMENTOUS   ALGAE beached smelts
                                                          OM

banished

light—

break—

waters' ZEBRA   MUSCLE *help* "toronto" [2]   ALL LONG THE SHORE
shores *peer*   *speck*   —GERONIMO   "garbage
                                          men striking
there CLOGGED THE PIPES'   BOATS' DEAD IN THE DOCK
helped its mosquitoes, kingfishers, man deemed *no*
mate wade   IN POOLS WHERE THEY BRED
now—

---

[2] constraints—seen from barker

nor a diner
that survives

dreams' coffee, French

SOMERSET coalstack freed om
no dream
fry a barge enters the lake
special Can pay a tax

witnessing every day permit

billow in sun parts of a process of the
9 hours away, alien ginkgo leaf abounds
fad for sidewalks [3]

[redacted] soon plucked the bird of the spirit. [redacted] soon killed the belief in the spirit. But not the practice. The practice continued with a sarcastic vehemence. [redacted] with a perfect inner contempt for the spirit and the consciousness of man, practices the same spirituality and universal love and [redacted] all the time, incessantly, like a drug habit. And inwardly gives not a fig for it. Only for the sensation. The pretty-pretty sensation of love, loving all the world. And the nice fluttering aeroplane sensation of [redacted] [redacted] Then the prettiest of all sensations, the sensation of [redacted] Oh, what a lot they understand, the darlings! So good at the trick, they are. Just a trick of self-conceit.

---

[3] old glory
zero's blooming excursion

2001 LITTLE DREAM OF WEDDINGS ALREADY PERFORMED [4]

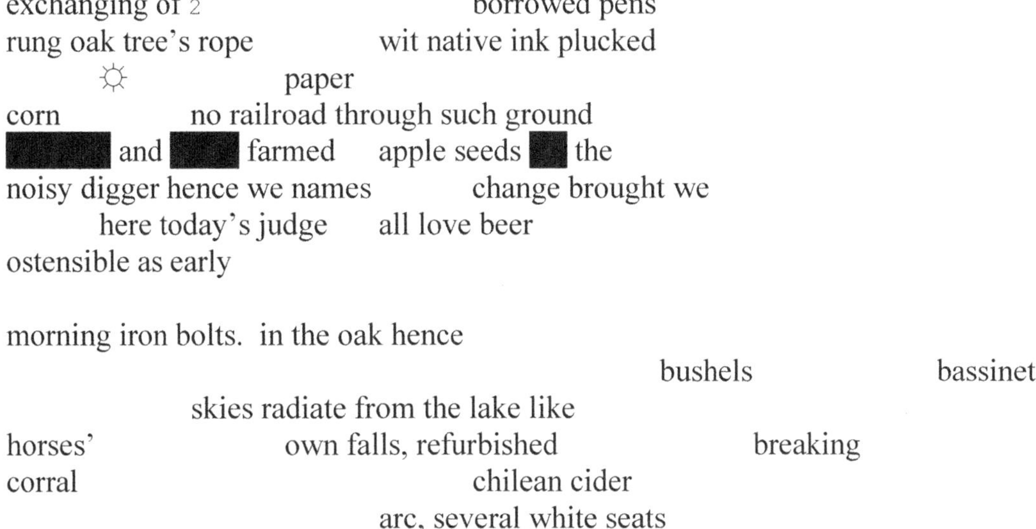

exchanging of 2   borrowed pens
rung oak tree's rope   wit native ink plucked
       ☼   paper
corn   no railroad through such ground
▮▮▮▮ and ▮▮▮ farmed   apple seeds ▮ the
noisy digger hence we names   change brought we
       here today's judge   all love beer
ostensible as early

morning iron bolts. in the oak hence
                                 bushels   bassinet
          skies radiate from the lake like
horses'   own falls, refurbished   breaking
corral   chilean cider
          arc, several white seats

after 27 years Betty Rubble debuts Flintstone vitamin; Curaeao gaining limited form of self rule Status Aparte; U.S. budget crisis fourth month; Clinton approves resumption of many government operations; "Father" opens Criterion Theater New York City 52 performances; coach Don Shula announcing retirement; Muralitharan no-balled for throwing in ODI vs. WI Gabba; $65.2 million British lottery 3 winners 2-3-4-13-42-44; 16th United Negro College Fund raising $12,600,000; "Crazy after You" closes Shubert Theater New York City 1622 performances; blizzard buries eastern U.S. at least 50 deaths; 1st time in 25 years no one elected to Baseball Hall of Fame; Israel frees some Palestinians; Chile signs treaty with UK and Northern Ireland for the Promotion and Protection of Investments with Protocol amidst ongoing disputes over Antarctica land claims while Iron Maiden plays live; Spanish court indicts General Augusto Pinochet; Jimmy Johnson announcing a new coach Miami Dolphins; Space Shuttle STS-72 Endeavour 10 launches; Russian troops arriving in Bosnia to joint U.S. operations; "Holiday" closes Circle in Square Theater New York City 49 performances; Liselotte Neumann Chrysler-Plymouth Tournament of Golf Champions; "Swinging On a Star" closes Music Box Theater New York City 97 performances; baseball owners unanimously approving inter-league play; Lisa Marie Presley New York divorcing Michael Jackson; NHL approving Winnipeg Jets' move to Phoenix; 46th NHL All-Star Game East beats West 5-4 Fleet Center Boston; Australia defeats Sri Lanka 2-0 World Series Cup; U.S. Female Figure Skating Michelle Kwan; WPAT FM New York City radio station switching to English-Spanish; 53rd Golden Globes Mel Gibson Nicole Kidman John Travolta; Karrie Webb LPGA HealthSouth Inaugural Golf Tournament; U.S. male Figure Skating Rudy Galindo; Chris Cairns scores 120 96 balls 10x4 9x6 Test New Zealand vs. Zim; Senate ratifies major arms reduction treaty; "Les Miserables" opens Music Hall Theatre Duisburg; 15 day-old siamese twins separated; Sarah Morales survives Sarahi dies; 70th Australian Women's Tennis Open Monica Seles beats Anke Huber 64 61; Catherine Roskam 1st New York female Episcopal bishop; France nuclear testing Muruora Island; Germany 1st Holocaust Remembrance Day; Shiv Chanderpaul scoring 303 Guyana vs. Jamaica Kingston; 84th Australian Men's Tennis Boris Becker beats M. Chang 62 64 26 62; "Hello Dolly!" closes Lunt-Fontanne Theater New York City 118 performances; Super Bowl XXX Dallas Cowboys beat Pittsburgh Steelers 27-17 Tempe Arizona; Super Bowl MVP; France ending nuclear tests; 23rd American Music Award Garth Brooks; 6,138th performance "Cats" London surpassing Broadway's longest-running "A Chorus Line"; last day Test cricket for David Boon

---

73 dead Sri Lankan suicide bombing; Ali Landry 22 Louisiana 45th Miss USA; NFL Pro Bowl NFC beats AFC 20-13; Heidi Fleiss beginning 7 year jail sentence; NFL Cleveland allows Art Modell to move franchise to Baltimore; leaves Browns' name behind; WYNY-FM New York City changing calls to WKTU-FM; IBM's Deep Blue defeats Gary Kasparov; 46th NBA All-Star Game East beats West 129-118 San Antonio Texas; Howard Stern will be making film "Private Parts"; Iroquois Bancorp won't disclose $1.1 million pre-tax loss on the sale of certain classified commercial mortgage loans; "Rent" opens off-Broadway; Yankee Energy sells its interest in Iroquois Pipeline; Gary Kirsten 188 for South Africa vs. UAE Rawalpindi; 1st full ODI for Netherlands Cricket World Cup vs. New Zealand; Nolan Clarke ODI debut Netherlands age 47; 1st full ODI for Kenya Cricket World Cup vs. India; Daytona 500; Tendulkar 127 India's Cricket World Cup vs. Kenya; Howard Stern Radio Show premieres York Pennsylvania WQXA 105.7 FM; Soyuz TM-23 launches orbit; Halle Berry divorcing David Justice; "Bus Stop" opens Circle in Square Theater New York City 29 performances; STS-75 Columbia 19 launches orbit; Mark Waugh 130 World Cup vs. Kenya; 207 with brother Steve; Rajindra Dhanraj taking 9-97 for Trinidad vs. Leeward Islands; Cuba downs 2 U.S. planes; Meg Mallon LPGA Cup o' Noodles Hawaiian Ladies' Golf Open; "Father" closes Criterion Theater New York City 52 performances; Rajindra Dhanraj taking 16-167 for Trinidad vs. Leeward Islands; Mark Waugh 126 World Cup vs. India; 38th Grammy Awards "Jagged Little Pill" Alanis Morisette; Kenya defeats West Indies all out 93 Cricket World Cup

UN EMPLOYED SKY PEOPLE *brutality every thing*
alarms, begin the news.

KARAHKWA

YOTAHALA [5]

explodes "under the sun
during the day a voice *his own*

grackles "under the stars' night *sleep*
neighbors TEHALIHWÁKHWA

"such times GE:GENH *for*
in earth

▯ ▯ which he'd

like whose bowels trees
round whose heart, deliver

eye 35   VERMONT, RATKÁHTHUHS
neighbor's   neighbor's   neighbor

RA'NWĘ'È:RĘH *for the goodness*
farts quiet

---

[5] 2001, thinking back, "that one busy highway"
the myth itself's its footnote

as the mouse "sun off moon
lit" ÚSKA

◻ ◻

technological centers of earth else it can't awake one phallus's 35
VERMONT ("big window") To convert

to a dawn's
approach *a bug*

caught in its webs screen
convert dawn

◻ ◻

still cracking Windowsills ("threshold"
never counts to go out (YOTAHALA. KARAHKWA.

nor he's in his dreams if
not for the sun

of the day, Lockport's Work, could have been visible
not for profit thereby he'd zip his pants
CHÍR or GÍS

we're stalling
He takes up its "razor"
now combing, his head OJI:TGWA:' we're

stalling UCHI'TKWÁHNEH

HO:NHGWEH

AGO:NHGWEH

fogged like something burns' star, dim, effect   HATËNOTHA'
35 VERMONT (its "little

☼ + ♂
mirror

▯ dice May YAKUKWÉ *round* this *morning's*
belly he'll return to this later

-ish, showers DELPHI ("bankrupt")("scabs") INC ensuing—

                       world, "not my job" [6]

like most wages
insides, don't ruin it

reflecting   JË:STA'Ë:
on the neighbors unfairly

reasonable, confidence
Φ [7]   *electroencephalography*

▯ ▯   I:SE:K

(swallowing. "catatonia.")

---

come to his window
interview *the earliest hummingbird*

"This one he'd walk to the stiff edge of the cliff," (you don't say: HO:NHGWEH)
something around ███████ lit
looks

awake unzipping
soft

part of his skull   ("infant wound")
alights   ("silks")

nowhere   GA:GWA:'
awaiting its moon.

2001 A MAN ON THE DUMP
HIS STORY'S HIS OTHER ONE

modes of the intertextual and appropriative seam its ecology's instances

doubled entendres: "a working people's culture":

> The secret of the human condition is that there is no equilibrium between man and the surrounding forces of nature, which infinitely exceed him when in inaction; there is only equilibrium in action by which man recreates his own life through work...produces his own natural existence. Through science he recreates the universe by means of...Through art he recreates the alliance between his body and his...It is to be noticed that each of these three things is something poor, empty and vain taken by itself and not in relation to the two others.

The two tasks of a society with its work in mind are "to individualize machinery" and "to individualize science." Open, "popularize," and reclaim them, individualizing the means of production must free workers from their corporate apparati while realizing the dignity of labor. It's impressive, how this template for our restoration is inscribed with the irrational:

> Disgust is the burdensomeness of our time. To acknowledge it to ourselves without giving way under it makes us mount upwards [or upon, depending how you look at it]. Disgust in all its forms is one of the most precious trials sent to man as a ladder by which to rise. I have a very larger share of this favour. We have to turn all our disgust into a disgust for ourselves...experience in the most exhausting manner the phenomenon of finality rebounding like a ball...work in order to eat, to eat in order to work. If we regard one of the two as an end, or the one and the other taken separately, we are lost. Only the cycle...

Taking this idea of "disgust for ourselves," and the "cycle" in what body should be the object of this disgust, together with an idea developed later, "he must either be detached or fall to the vegetative level," one can arrive at some ideas about her own practice. If it is somehow a work of world-making, and if one "recreates his own life through work," then expunging maintainable identity formations with "disgust" and the laborious, objective ("detached") sensibility to how one may "eat" by that (as if something from the east, to not have to eat) maybe knows what material has been pulsing with the difficulty. To entertain the "individualized science and machinery"—to spotlight her individual against the commune? [8] ▮▮▮▮ emphasizes her "cycle"—where that finds shape is its ▮▮▮▮▮▮ sharing their environments produces things—"taken separately" &c.

---

[8] and as the text, a chain letter
"I fear not what man can do unto me"

boomerang effect bucket lists or one's ~~ought~~ not to talk or act as if it were asleep

maintain space   ~~one~~

the dog's intelligence being decided
a shock   becomes human
being learned

two's

where is my
haven't seen it
where is you
might check over
where i said
haven't seen it

three's

spillway slips something
push   in

four's

like consciousness, adds, buried
the thing in the mouth
gradually, we drove trucks
would bury our
█ is useless

five's

coyote sticks his ███ in everything

six's

seven's

Or don't ma
only's playing
talk, back

eight's

wolved, with hoofs no less what else
did you call
hungrier nostril

grooms nine

it'd give its limb to farm
sheep no
rubber

(███ *taken*)

fuck <u>me</u>

ten's

                                           trunks bleed south of the equator

Chagall hung behind the computer.   mercury

     lasered in the wood. been thinking   this soul-frame is no jellyfish
           to erase the caption. all it wanted   barreled in bacon fat
       a green man stairs at the goat   caddies him, down with you
      the milk made in its head   hailing its thief
      him bearing the sprig   immortal herds, a pan
        gifts from Chuck I   's phallus swallowed by a school to
      smashed Pat's Mollie   render it confined
        could turn nonplused I   to ivy, men, hemoglobin
                               ain't ridden his truck in three years

                                                  (

ride
    the Bull rides

12 13 and 1st crush:

█████'s p

cleave us alone [9]

)

DREAMCATCHERS

to peace pipe

... ...

seventeen's

poster **and with ma's own signature, released**

seventeens

paris PEH—WEE [10]
of the island [11]

---

[9] the dog "████████████████████ no place to spit but in his face."
[10] "They laugh at me / but I'm not laughed at"

[11] USMC 1996; Ilmurran.

Lenny Wilkens winningest coach 1,000[th] NBA victory; introducing toll-free 888 area code; Gladiator re-opening Copeland swimming pool; Tendulkar 137 India Cricket World Cup losing to Sierra Leone; 26th Easter Seal Telethon; Auckland beats Wellington by 9 wickets Shell Trophy Final; suicide bomber kills 59 Israel; Bob Dole sweeping Republican primaries; Earl Weaver Jim Bunning Hall of Fame; 10th American Comedy Award; 2nd Blockbuster Entertainment Awards; Aravinda De Silva 145 Sri Lanka vs. Kenya Cricket World Cup; Kandy 5-398 in 50 overs; 1st surface Pluto photos Hubble Space Telescope; British Steel Workington winning Lithuanian multi-million pound order; Magic Johnson 2nd NBA player 10,000 career assists; Javed Miandad's last international Pak's WC QF loss to India; Jayasuriya 82 off 44 balls 13x4 3x6 vs. England WC QF; STS-75 Columbia 19 landing; 22nd People's Choice Awards "Apollo 13" Tom Hanks; Mayor Guiliani visiting Israel; Chris Harris 130 losing New Zealand vs. Australia World Cup; Mark Waugh 110 vs. New Zealand for his third century in World Cup; Leeward Islands beat Trinidad by 73 runs Red Stripe Trophy; Sri Lanka beats India World Cup semi as riots stop play; Thomas Hamilton kills 16 kindergarteners their teacher and himself; Australia beats West Indies by 5 runs in amazing cricket World Cup semi; Crufts show NEC Birmingham 1995 winner Joshua an Irish setter; Aravinda De Silva 107 and 3-42 Cricket World Cup; "Bus Stop" closes Circle in Square Theater New York City 29 performances; "Getting Away With Murder" opens Broadhurst New York City 17 performances; Liselotte Neumann wins LPGA Ping/Welch's Golf Championship; Mike Tyson KOs Frank Bruno 3rd round; gains Heavyweight title; Montreal Canadian's 1st game new arena; Sri Lanka beats Australia 7 wickets World Cup; 50,000 swimmers raise $15 million BT's Swimathon '96; Winnie Mandela divorcing Nelson after 38 years; Britain alarmed cow disease; Erik and Lyle Menendez found guilty of killing parents; "Love Thy Neighbor" opens Booth Theater New York City; U.K. admits humans can catch CJD Mad Cow Disease; "Night of the Iguana" opens Criterion Theater New York City 68 performances; UN tribunal charges war crimes by Bosnian Muslims and Croats; Cheryl Depew Florida 13th Miss Hawaiian Tropic International; STS-76 Atlantis 16 launches orbit; 16th Golden Raspberry Awards Showgirls; "Eastenders" star Michael French reported homosexual; Laura Davies wins LPGA Standard Register Ping Golf Tournament; Metropolitan Transportation Authority raising New York City bridge tolls $3.50 each way; 68th Academy Awards "Braveheart" Nicholas Cage Susan Sarandon; Comet C/1996 B2 Hyakutake approaching within 0.1018 AUs of Earth; Freedom Shoemakers closing on Maryport's Solway Estate; Ice Dance Championship Edmonton Gritshuk and Platov; Ice Pairs Championship Edmonton Eltsova and Bushkov; Ladies' Figure Skating Championship Edmonton Michelle Kwan; Men's Figure Skating Championship Edmonton Todd Eldredge; U.S. issuing new $100 bill; Last day 1st class cricket Allan Border Qld vs. Vic; "State Fair" opens Music Box Theater New York City 118 performances; "7 Guitars" opens Walter Kerr Theater New York City; Katie Beam 17 Oklahoma 35th Miss Teenage America; 10th Soul Train Music Awards Patti Labelle Boyz II Men; Cleveland Browns re-named Baltimore Ravens; New York Yankees beat New York Mets 7-3 exhibition game; Lara 146 cricket not out in ODI vs. New Zealand Port-of-Spain; New York Mets beat New York Yankees 5-3 exhibition game; Prince Edward and girlfriend Sophie visiting Graystoke Castle; 15th NCAA Women's Basketball Championship Tennessee beats Georgia 83-65; 1st Opening Day in history in March Seattle; 25th Nabisco Dinah Shore Golf Championship Patty Sheehan; "Getting Away With Murder" closes Broadhurst New York City 17 performances; Karnataka defeats Tamil Nadu 1st inning Ranji Trophy; "Midsummer Night's Dream" opens Lunt-Fontanne New York City 66 performances; Radio Canada International's final shortwave broadcast; Space Shuttle STS-76 Atlantis 16 lands; Wrestlemania XII Shawn Michaels beats Brett Hart for WWF title

IN CREE THERE IS NO WORD FOR HELLO

The fox learned how to cross the road.

ii doubtful as he who sees [12] thru dusky night

                             [13] thinks he sees the moon's uncertain light

---

[12] muscles and wombs
they needn't have had faces at all
[13] beautiful to thought as it had
been present bodily
sense and caesuras

medicalization of the 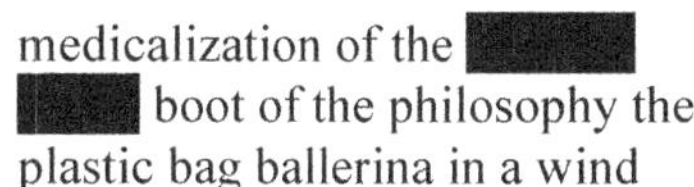
boot of the philosophy the
plastic bag ballerina in a wind

half its window's [14]

sand

~~INVECTIVES~~
long-term security
         the body in
the body **her gladness bruised** the tired
in transport **the good** morning
arc sponged **away from imbibing** its excess
~~color determined by scarlet~~

---

[14] when speaking of production, commodities appear at first sight an extremely obvious, trivial thing.

remember the ▮▮▮▮ and the unprecedented squabble when they cast a
in the midst of their nap a load of ▮▮▮▮ this made it to every cover
almost lost their funding

Aoidē "Day" re

context "intend   to do what I want to do and be whom

I want to be answering only to ▮▮▮▮   contemporary

move mints his and her Bitch Philosophy" a way

that's genuine, to one's own generation" as "The Day of the Barbarians" or

"Muhammad" by or   " 'S dying to show you"   *recent publications her*

logic Meletē front line "

snark, intends to scream shout race the engines call

when we feel like it throw

the tantrums in Bloomingdale's seats of the body cast "famine

fed   "Propaganda"

Mnēmē singing

Hold his hand (though I can't see he deserves
forgiveness. There are these necessities
are bigger than we are.

▮▮▮▮▮▮ ignition   TV alight on what torched and freed [15]

umbrella om wells lit and wandering, desert, washed eleven O clocks whom

BLOG sees me on

---

[15] science of ballyhoo, nephew brings uncle sigmund to the pythia:
"Group of Girls Puff at Cigarettes as Gesture of ▼

“everyone’s project”

GROT well's cream, voluminous shelf, pump's me later

▲ sprung from uranus and gaia

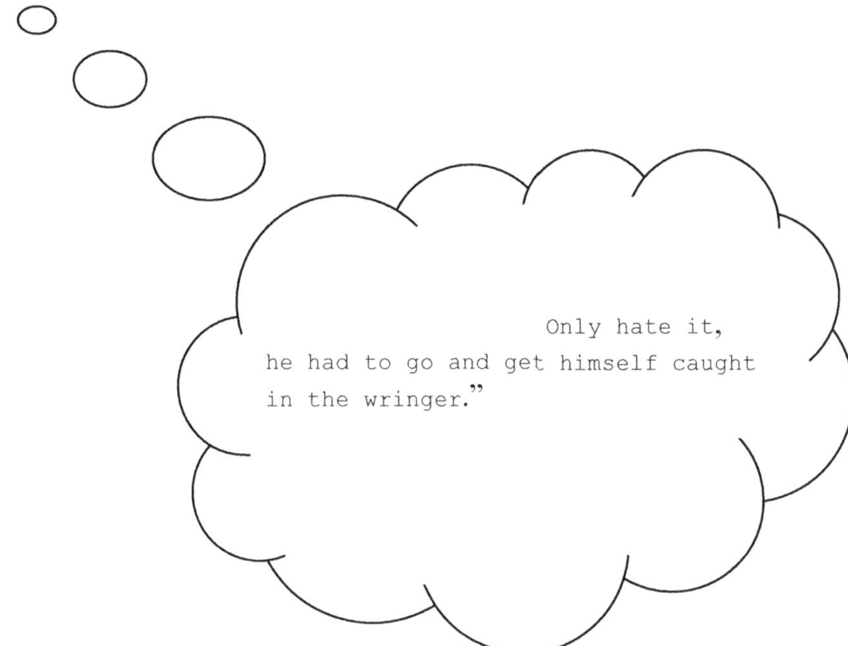

[16] cast out burning oils my honey heard me

comin I saw Jody runnin like

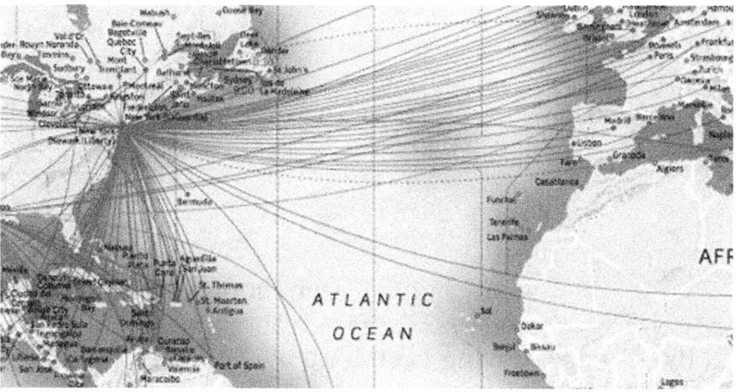

2 enlistments to pan grind there ain't no use in goin

back Jody's livin it up in the shack

slathered and rinsed, logged, clean-shaven

~~grind and shores that doesn't matter the pathetic~~
library that contained ~~perhaps not one voluminous distinction must go down also~~
by defect of virtue that ~~it~~ contains nothing of you
       collection of books from *liber,* gen. *libri* "book, paper, parchment" originally "the inner
        bark of trees" probably derivative of **leub(h)-* "to strip, to peel" see
                    leaves ~~as the freak day was shared~~

              I dominate this space [17]

          seen though, by its own light
~~like fencing having been for a season~~   successful
all those fences having been for a
     ~~UNITS~~   lot,
some nerve, rent, toss another
         dare lined by wires and trees under the street

~~INVECTIVES~~

Iris and its ewer come [18]

                          to don't **then it appeared**

                        elusive speak she will [21]

                          say, don't be **a lost star**

                       finding its path pissed,

                            ask **so it burned**

                  beyond all measure [you] [sleep]

☼

---

[17] @ 7 years old: "I agree to think of myself as a beautiful p

[18] Iris carried an ewer. The bus's driver, at 2 in the morning, arriving with them, through a swamp, she has instructions to go around in circles, so that they are lost. The barbers, waiting, are male civilians. Scalps. Paris Island is in the Carolinas. See much later.

[19] old glory ~~him~~

~~were carried abroad~~ talk [20]

fans, over the shelf

---

[20] + ~~her~~

sea shanty you had a good home but you left
you had a good home but you left [21]
2001

1996 58th NCAA Men's Basketball Championship Kentucky beats Syracuse 76-67; Sri Lanka 9-349 50 overs beats Pakistan 315 all out; Singapore Jayasuriya hits ton in 48 balls world ODI record Singapore; Tigers' Cecil Fielder steals 1st base in 1,097[th] career game; Commerce Secretary Ronald Brown killed plane crash; FBI arrests Unabomber; South Australia grab draw vs. WA Sheffield Shield; St. Francis Fighting Saints college baseball run record 71-1; Howard Stern Radio Show premiering Austin Texas KJFK 98.9 FM; "Inherit the Wind" opens Royale Theater New York City 45 performances; John Bobbitt under house arrest Las Vegas 120 days; Albert Belle hits Sports Illustrated photographer Tony Tomsic in the hand prior to game; 8th Seniors' Golf Tradition Jack Nicklaus; Kelly Robbins Sacramento 12 Bridges LPGA Golf Classic; Pakistan beats Sri Lanka Singer Cup Singapore; Bruce Seldon TKOs Tony Tucker in 7 winning vacated WBA boxing title; Detroit Red Wings 2nd NHL team winning 60 games in 1 season; Clinton signs line-item veto bill; blocks ban on late-term abortions; "King and I" premieres Neil Simon Theater New York City 781 performances; en route to NHL record 62 victories Detroit Red Wings win 61; Ottawa Senators eliminate Stanley Cup Champs New Jersey Devils; 60th Golf Masters Championship Nick Faldo 276; "Apple Doesn't Fall" opens Lyceum Theater New York City 1 performance; Detroit Red Wings NHL record 62 games; 100th Boston Marathon Moses Tanui Kenya 2:09:15.9; 25th Boston Women's Marathon Uta Pippig Germany 2:27:12.6; "Apple Doesn't Fall" closes Lyceum Theater New York City 1 performance; "Funny Thing Happened" opens St. James Theater New York City 715 performances; Rangers score 16 in 8th vs. Orioles; South Africa defeats Pakistan Pepsi Cup Sharjah; Chicago Bulls record 72 victories in 1 season; 57th PGA Seniors' Golf Championship Hale Irwin; Barb Mucha LPGA Chick-fil-A Charity Golf Championship; Chicago Bulls NBA record 72-8; "Delicate Balance" opens Plymouth Theater New York City; Matabeleland beats Mashonaland Country District Logan Cup; Wayne James scoring 99 and 99 and ct 11 stp 2 Logan Cup Final; Howard Stern Radio Show premieres Reno Nevada KRZQ 96.5 FM; Sotheby begins 4 day auctioning Jackie Onassis nets $34.5 million; 31st Academy of Country Music Awards Shania Twain; highest scoring baseball game in 17 years Twins 24 Tigers 11; "Jack-Night on Town with John Barrymore" opens Belasco 12 performances; "Bring in Da Noise, Bring in Da Funk" opens Ambassador Theater New York City; Shaun Pollock takes 4 wickets in 4 balls for Warwickshire B&H; Sotheby ending 4 day auctioning Jackie O. $34.5 million; Brunswick World Tournament of Champions Dave D'Entremont; "Big" opens Shubert Theater New York City 193 performances; Martin Bryant shooting 35 Port Arthur Tasmania; Meg Mallon LPGA Sara Lee Golf Classic; Howard Stern Radio Show premieres Fresno California KFRR 104.1 FM; "Rent" opens Nederlander Theater New York City; "Buried Child" opens Atkinson Theater New York City 77 performances; Dutch/Italian Beppo-SAX launch Cape Canaveral; Operation Grapes of Wrath and the shelling of Qana; Howard Stern Radio Show premieres Grand Ra̶ ̶ ̶ FM wind pipes ~~were~~ assisting

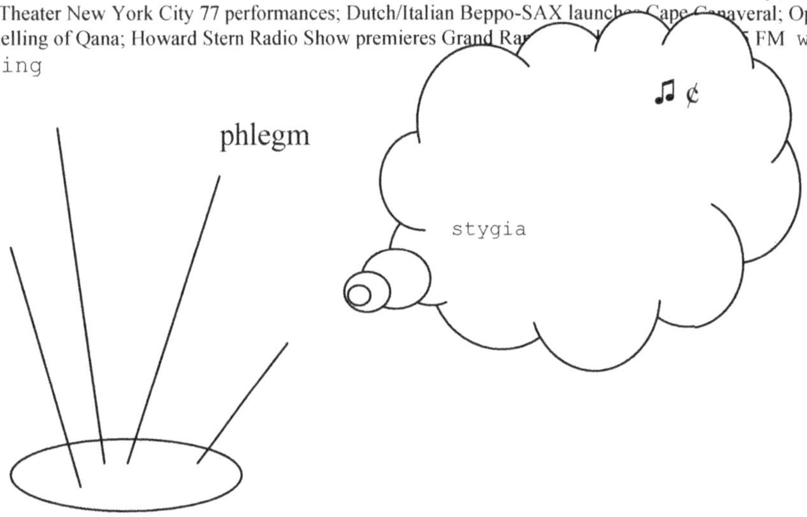

phlegm

stygia

---

[21] a yellow bird with a yellow bill
was sittin on my windowsill
i lured him in with a piece of bread
and then i smashed his little head

dry as the seed gathered in the soil
watered
the grass grew in drawn grasses watered
like little notions ~~going on to~~
and speaking
affair's little notion's phrasing
corners each
bends grain in the spoke sur
prise the fair
stall to my
child's cotton
candy sur
prise wherever ~~grows~~
~~on up~~ his
ribbon's pulled like cotton ~~candied~~
yards from
some mouth look
such
swallowed color! here's your dollar
pick your duck ~~and think~~ barraged
hawker of one
still ~~struggling~~ ok
ok another dollar
~~in bondage~~ are
these things like
waiting, paraded
like pigs and cows
this morning's ~~sponsored~~
almost over plastics tag the ears' still touch
~~time~~ us the ribbon will
~~end i do~~ not fear parades
for the school's dried lunch which you know
almost over is ~~not~~
not pops trade
the seed
to water in the
grind if we
fill you for

parched, would
pocket, known
how each broke

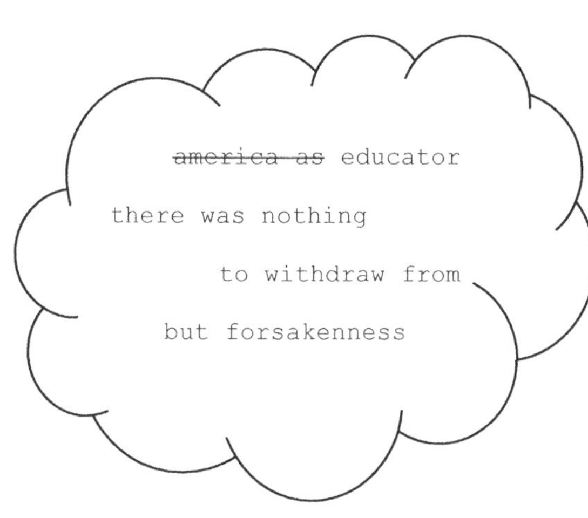

acrobat
~~does not do~~
flips for you
…

…at this point the persona must understand that he's on the 2002, late

POOR MOUSE, DUST, AND WHAT SHOULD HAVE STAYED IN ITS HOLE [23]

venue, wires, Chryses

Arrivals, all over again no question, what will happen
Questions his opener must mark the place, the body that
They come to, has arrived there
Trick attractions let's hum ingested it

---

[23] I used to sleep at the foot of old glory

☼

overhead now. You'll have to kill him. Too low. remember
Camouflaged (and loud) "cargo" their conference, on the map all our dates
that like constellations
eye, in the news

Host, *
Premier Camping
sand-blown, generous

* never even got him soup

Kevan James 103 takes 4 wickets in 4 balls Hants vs. Ind; NHL Winnipeg Jets turning Phoenix Coyotes; Placido Domingo new art director Washington Opera; WBSI TV replacing WNYC on channel 31 New York City; Boris Yeltsin reelected Russia; Hotmail e-mail service beginning; A's score 13 in 1st vs. Angels; New York Yankee John Weteland ties Lee Smith's record 19 consecutive saves; 103rd Wimbledon Women's Tennis Graf beats Vicaro 63 75; Yankee John Weteland sets record 20th consecutive save en route to 24; 110th Wimbledon Men's Tennis Krajicek beats Washington 63 64 63; 17th U.S. Seniors' Golf Open Dave Stockton; Joan Pitcock LPGA Jamie Farr Kroger Golf Classic; Space Shuttle STS-78 Columbia 20 lands; 67th All-Star Baseball NL wins 6-0 Veterans Stadium; All-Star MVP Mike Piazza Los Angeles Dodgers; U.S. Senate approving 90-cent raise to minimum wage; Kirby Puckett retiring Minnesota Twins; Michael Jordan signing NBA contract 1 year $25 million; 1st Super 8's tournament Kuala Lumpur; Charles and Diana agreeing to divorce; Cigar record 16th straight win ties Citation from 1940; 14th Seniors' Players Golf Championship Raymond Floyd; "How To Succeed in Business..." closes Rodgers New York City 548 performances; Michelle McGann Youngstown-Warren LPGA Golf Classic; New York Yankee John Weteland sets record 24 consecutive saves; 1st time Yankees sweep complete season series in Baltimore; "Thousand Clowns" opens Criterion Theater New York City 32 performances; after 2,216 consecutive games at shortstop Cal Ripkin going to 3rd; MSNBC beginning Microsoft internet-NBC TV; Charles and Di signing divorce papers; southern Mexico 6.5 earthquake; 230 people aboard 747 TWA 800 crashing off Long Island; Yank John Weteland blows save after record 24 consecutive saves; Ireland beats Netherlands 1st European Championship Final; Jason Gallian 312 in 683 minutes for Lancashire vs. Derbyshire; XXVI Olympic games opening Atlanta Georgia; 125th British Golf Open Tom Lehman 271 Royal Lytham; Dottie Pepper LPGA Friendly's Golf Classic; Wayne Gretzky signing 2 year deal New York Rangers; Kim LaPlante Washington state crowned Mrs. United States; bomb mars Summer Olympic games Atlanta; David Sales 210 on 1st class cricket debut for Northants vs. Worcs; New York Yankee Darryl Strawberry 300 homers; Vicki Fergon LPGA Micelob Light Heartland Golf Classic; Tommy Lasorda retiring manager Los Angeles Dodgers

ANOTHER MATTER COME to minus degree
nylon snowmen deflate. His hairdryer's impotent
as well extension
chord's lazy

whirring gears of a jingle box. For ████████
yards dictate their street. By autumn the red turning
plots fallow, candle light gravy all the innards
kept we've memories. Light like berries
with hat removed
strung

to be there. Bloodless cousins eggnog
wave to the moon, unasked heat's divvied

the bed potential. ▮ she's visiting

brushed her teeth leaves cookies before her
quilt's

already somebody's old

trunk. Potential not
moth ball, locked. as

All through town snow

blackened.
had fallen, soft bone, woods
bricks fired, chimney leaning

straightens herself, wiping hands, grandma's old tablecloth smooth now each
place set. At four o'clock she untied her apron
pouring her drink with creamy
windows, where planes of wire crisscross through branches

stitching the place together. The hearth stone tender no
stone, brined in ma's math
tub a turkey, dinner a street

berried up and down by dusks mute gray and reaching
smokes, penned
yard's

For the ██████ there had been a decline of which it was their miserable fate never to know, while they raised their holy incantations. These are not the great flower of the spirit. Purged by hard experience (worn bodies from which a white dove springs), they are not all ████ as they and we have imagined. Bodily suffering was more an alleviation than otherwise, a distraction that kept them mercifully blinded. They were condemned to be without flower, to sow themselves basely that after them others might know the end. Each shrank from an imagination that would sever him from the rest.

---

[24] Her joy in it changes the ██████████████ to harmless jealousy, and she is left alone.

something for drawing shared
lines in sand things
wake dream
and vote—Mars digitized they do. Collateral lambs brought [26]

skin to get allergic things laid first where ███ rolls the sky's
such such a reef at night Milky
Way all so fresh, when finding fresh reefs land

go elastic their hotdogs splitting autumn. Football and grass sports up
north 7 or 9 kinds of snow telescopic stations up there using a very advanced
refrigerator—sands, the opposite—letter, clothes on

the way, through
him submarines, smuggling a picnic oxygen,

him ribbons, round trees, him bone's
meat, earth-ish
washing gear, oiled, saggy lingeries

records—then policy, podium, theatre, almanac
global weathering shtick him

molting, fingerprint, mars

---

[25] my return home is gone. but my glory shall be everlasting
[26] on the ███ of our own divided psyche

departing, smoke herring, no one's brought anis what
will be done parenthetical New Year's thing
Jon would perform in through the front look
out your back [27]

screen door, moon neighbors, always full surfacing him in view of the sulfur
their hair drains—view
of their canal

glass and her
and a wedge of lime

light like a berry
their summer'd watched

basil dig—probably seeing
something tells
him to remember, via satellite

send words? Back?

filed—sleeve it'd worn, offer her
it'd whittled for eggnog toothpick stirs her martini olive a region'd
bunkering down—fireplace
fingerprint

---

[27] large mammal

MTV launching 2nd TV channel M2; Clinton signs bill raising minimum wage; Congress passing welfare reform bill; 24th du Maurier Golf Classic Laura Davies; 26th Olympic Games closing Atlanta; Bunning Weaver Foster and Hanlon inducted Hall of Fame; Dallas Cowboys playing Kansas City Chiefs Monterrey Mexico; NASA announces life may have existed on Mars; Bob Dole picking Jack Kemp as Republican Vice Presidential running mate; Dare and Go ending Cigar's record tying victory streak at 16; Parlisha Williams Louisiana crowned Ms. Black U.S.A.; new Metroplex opens Buffalo New York; Yankees lose ending 3rd best home series victory streak at 24; 78th PGA Championship Mark Brooks 277 Vallhalla Golf Club Kentucky; Emilee Klein LPGA Ping Welch's Golf Championship; "Thousand Clowns" closes Criterion Theater New York City 32 performances; Republican convention opening San Diego; Microsoft releasing Internet Explorer 3.0; Bob Dole and Jack Kemp nominated; Soyuz TM-24 launches orbit; Emilee Klein LPGA Weetabix Women's British Golf Open; record 6,654 taps at Macy's New York Tap-o-mania; India defeats Pakistan Under-15 World Challenge Final at Lord's; Christie Lee Woods 18 Texas 14th Miss Teen USA; "Hughie" opens Circle in Square Theater New York City; new Netscape Browser 3.0; 96th U.S. Golf Amateur Championship Tiger Woods; Clinton approving welfare reform bill; Laura Davies Star Bank LPGA Golf Classic; Democrats convening Chicago; Liam Botham takes 5-67 on 1st class debut Hants vs. Middlesex; Iraqis strike Kurdish enclave

tomorrow   yesterday   dunes

in media re   s

[28] shards and dust   export

mingle Jerry Lewis' 31st Muscular Dystrophy telethon $49,200,000 Michelle McGann LPGA where are the grackles

State Farm Rail Golf Classic Soyuz TM-24 lands after you were dragging a trunk to make me a bridge warning
U.S. attacking Iraq's southern air defenses 13th MTV Video Music we played minor gods Awards Alanis Morrisette Smashing

all day Pumpkins

"Summer and Smoke" opens Criterion Theater New York City Baltimore Orioles' Eddie Murray's 500th career home run 110th U.S.
Women's Tennis Steffi Graf beats Monica Seles least it won't be as bad as having to kill that bunny

75 64 116th U.S. Men's Tennis Pete Sampras beats Michael Chang 61 64 76 48th Emmy Awards ER dry, scoured, purple
crow Dennis Franz Kathy Baker "7 Guitars" closes Walter Kerr Theater New York City this, your morning's Dottie Pepper
Safeway LPGA Ping-Cellular One LPGA Golf Championship Sri Lanka defeats Australia true

count Singer World Series Colombo Phil Simmons 171 taking 6-14 for Leics vs. Durham Iraq how did you earn your
living, how did you earn your pay halts attacks on U.S. planes enforcing flight exclusion zones in north and south A's
Mark McGwire 13th that side, global bird, the bills due

player hitting 50 home runs in 1 season Dean Headley taking 3rd cricket when our ████████ ceased working

hat-trick of season Kent vs. Hampshire New York Met Todd Huntley when all of the ████

whispering record 41 home runs by a catcher Tara Dawn Holland Kansas 23 70th Miss America a moment more please

2nd Presidents Golf wasn't ready Cup U.S. beats International team niagara
be water

16-15 meander Robert Jones Virginia Bangladesh beats UAE by 104 runs ACC Trophy Final a time she spends
scribbling Karrie Webb LPGA SAFECO Golf Classic Texas Rangers in the woods along the cliff that is a
shore retiring 1st number Nolan Ryan's 34 1st one-day international Canada India vs. Pakistan the shade must be good

Toronto Howard Stern Radio Show premieres Panama City Florida WTBB 97.7 FM
when shade stops by

what's remembered 1996 Twins' Paul Molitor 21st player reaching 3,000 hits Space Shuttle STS-79 Atlantis 17 launches Dodger
Hideo Nomo no-hits screaming over paper and no, crying out loud Colorado Rockies 9-0 Coors Field Roger
Clemens tying his own in her afternoon sun

---

[28] shrapnel the fine print see previous note on commodities

record 20 strikeouts "Skylight" opens still days but
Royale Theater New York City weedy slope, was there a rabbit
ditch

Christie Brinkley marrying 4th time and Peter Cook John F. Kennedy hard edge
sopped, ditch Jr. marrying Caroline Bisset 4th Solheim Cup U.S. beats Europe 17-11 St. Pierre Wales Howard Stern radio
mosquito

triage show premieres West Palm Beach Florida WCLB 95.5 FM Howard Stern radio show premieres Wilkes-Barre Pennsylvania
WZMT 97.9 FM violence flares in Jerusalem Israel opening tourist mumbling waking in its morning like the time
there wasn't we begin the story each tunnel

San Francisco Giant Bobby Bond 2nd player hitting 40 home runs stealing newspaper, street sleeper 40 bases

Space Shuttle STS-79 Atlantis 17 lands Baltimore Oriole Roberto Alomar spits in face my second body of umpire John

Hirschbeck Taliban captures Afghan capital 1st ODI played Kenya maybe could have used you home team

vs. Sri Lanka Joyce Giraud 8th Ms. Venus fresh paint Swimwear Nebraska like our small blue pills and Penn
State are sticking 5th and 6th major five months in, her third first, while my first and second
colleges winning 700 Yankee Jim Leyitz 2nd catcher wearing

"yow" when her boats go by shin hockey masks Orioles' Roberto Alomar suspended 5 games Troy Davis Iowa State
running deep no one faltering

378 yards 3rd highest in college football games others Michigan Notre Dame Texas Alabama pink rubber boot
leathers what's new 1996 8 and more years before his own 2005 International Oil Spill Conference 2003 field teams completed
3107 transects no more

blistering tan dug described and photographed 19515 trenches and collected 26158 samples for total petroleum hydrocarbon
(TPH) analysis 2802 samples for detailed chemical characterization and fingerprinting and 134 bivalve tissue samples

34th Tennis Fed Cup U.S.A. beating Spain Atlantic City 5-0 Alanis was i a man
or something

Morissette ending 1st U.S. tour Houston Texas Baltimore Orioles ending season record 257 past all that sea
palm salt glinting home runs

"Delicate Balance" closes Plymouth Theater New mangrove so our neighbors York City Houston

Astros retiring won't

Nolan Ryan's speak of me 34 Nintendo

slick 64 dredge it video game system debuting U.S.A. 3 months after Japan Oriole Brady Anderson 14th time 50 homers Browns' 1st game as Ravens U.S. winning Fed Cup our place was made i

theory as I see myself reflected in nature, I see in myself a reflection of nature **HINGE** [29] **GROT**

████ leaves little doubt that the terrain of history, in the sense of political conflict, is too implicated in the wars of self-interest to be a site for ethics like a negative theologian, ████ is most effective in characterizing what the grounds of our concern for the other are *not*

☼ glory

~~30th Country Music Association Award Brooks and Dunn; Thunderdome Tampa Bay renamed Tropicana Field; BPAA U.S. Bowling Open Dave Husted; BPAA U.S. Women's Bowling Open Liz Johnson; Shahid Afridi scoring century in 37 balls for Pakistan vs. Sri Lanka; Caroline Pierce LPGA JAL Big Apple Golf Classic; Cleveland Indians strike out 23 Baltimore Orioles 12-inning playoff game; Yankee Bernie Williams switch hitting home runs in post-season game; Bob Dole and Bill Clinton 1st debate; New York Jet Nick Lowrey tying Jan Stenerud 373 NFL field goals; Howard Stern releasing paperback book "Miss America"; Cornerstone dedication Holocaust Museum New York City; Ford buying rights to name Detroit dome stadium $40 million; Annika Sorenstam Betsy King Golf Classic; Ethnic violence Zairian refugee camps; Senate criminalizes economic espionage; "Big" closes Shubert Theater New York City 193 performances; New York Jet Nick Lowrey breaking Jan Stenerud NFL field goal record 374; Yankees 3 Orioles 3 combine to tie playoff record 6; Braves St. Louis 14-0 NLCS; Dow Jones 1st time closing over 6,000; Air Force admits foreign-language knowledge is key to global engagement strategy; combat ID tool provides better battle field picture; inspectors say no evidence to date on CIA drug link to contras; 6,010; Packer Chris Jacke kicks longest overtime-ending field goal; 53 yards; "Taking Sides" opens Atkinson Theater New York City; Braves beat Yankees by record-tying 11 runs World Series; Annika Sorenstam LPGA Samsung World Championship of Women's Golf; Braves Andruw Jones youngest player homering World Series; "Summer and Smoke" closes Criterion Theater New York City; Wasim Akram and Saqlain Mushtaq cricket Test record 313 for 8th wicket; Wasim Akram 257 vs. Zimbabwe Sheikhupura 12 sixes; refugees from Rwanda and Burundi abandoning camps; Yankee Bernie Williams hitting record-tying 7th post-season homer; Paige prods Lockheed Martin to integrate key C31 systems; Yankees tying record 6th straight post-season road win en route to 8; Yankees set record coming back 6-0 in World Series game to beat Atlanta Braves 8-6; also set record of 7th straight road win; Hasan Raza making Test cricket debut for Pakistan age 14 years 238 days; last game Atlanta County Fulton Stadium; Yankees winning record 8th straight road post-season win no loss; Frank brother of Yank manager Joe Torre heart transplant; Defense Secretary William Perry has removed controversial material from School of the Americas manuals; Horse Racing Breeders' Cup Champs Lit de Justice Storm Song Jewel Princess Da Hass Boston Harbor Pilsudski Alphabet Soup at Woodbine; Fox News Channel launches; U.S. beats Japan 21-14 Nichirei International Golf Tournament; Goa upsetting Karnataka winning 1st Ranji Cricket Trophy game ever~~

These characters are here expressed as belonging to the building; as belonging to the builder, they would be expressed thus: 1. Savageness or Rudeness. 2. Love of change. 3. Love of Nature. 4. Disturbed

---

[29] of the interconnectivity of the word matrix, therefore, of concepts and life experience, individually and in social groups, summarily promoting transcendence of the reader's i am

[30] of the core of thought processing the myth itself's its footnote it ████ the imagination which creates it retentive of past ████

Imagination. 5. Obstinacy. 6. Generosity. Dream, horror, that once woke up, who must make a tool of the creature, a man of him.

Gerald Williams 1st New York Yankee since 1934 6 hits 1 game; "Ideal Husband" opens Barrymore Theater New York City 308 performances; Martin Moxon and Michael Vaughan making 362 1st wickets Yorks vs. Glam; 122nd Kentucky Derby Jerry Bailey aboard Grindstone 2:01; ABC Bud Light Masters Bowling Tournament Ernie Schlegel; Greg Pavlik one-hits Tigers making Rangers 1st AL team pitching back-to-back one-hitters since Washington Senators 1917; "Jack-Night on Town with John Barrymore" closes Belasco 12 performances; Karrie Webb LPGA Sprint Titleholders Golf Championship; Renette Cruz Vancouver crowned Miss Canadian Universe; Alvaro Arzu aiming at ending 35-year civil war; Howard Stern Radio Show premieres Hartford Connecticut WCCC 106.9 FM; Comedian Martin Lawrence suffering nervous breakdown; New York Yankee Dwight Gooden wins 1st AL game beating Tigers 10-3; South Africa's Constitutional Assembly adopting post-apartheid constitution; 2 Marine helicopters colliding joint U.S. and British war games; "Twister" premieres; Florida Marlin Al Leiter no-hits Colorado Rockies 11-0; 109 people aboard Valujet DC-9 crashing in Everglades; 42nd McDonald's LPGA Championship Laura Davies; "Inherit the Wind" closes Royale Theater New York City 45 performances; "Night of the Iguana" closes Criterion Theater New York City 68 performances; Yankees losing 8-0 to Chicago White Sox come back to win 9-8; O. J. Simpson appearing on British TV discussing his not guilty verdict; New York Yankee Dwight Gooden no-hits Seattle Mariners 2-0; Sammy Sosa 1st Chicago Cub hitting 2 home runs in 1 inning; Alicia Machado 18 Venezuela 45th Miss Universe; Habib and Whitaker making 320 Leics vs. Worcs; 122nd Preakness Pat Day aboard Louis Quatorze wins 1:53.2; WIBC Bowling Queen Lisa Wagner; STS-77 Endeavour 11 launches orbit; blackout through Queens New York; Ken Griffey Jr. 26 8th youngest hitting 200 home runs; Red Sox Roger Clemens beats Yankees for his 200th win; Emmy 23rd Daytime Award Susan Lucci loses 16th time; "Tartuffe: Born Again" opens Circle in Square Theater New York City 29 performances; Fred Norris of Howard Stern show changing legal name to Eric; "Spy Hard" starring Leslie Nielsen released; Jennifer Maria Holsten 18 crowned Miss Filipino-American; Indianapolis 500; Laura Davies J C Penney/LPGA Skins Golf Game; "Midsummer Night's Dream" closes Lunt-Fontanne New York City 66 performances; Rosie Jones LPGA Corning Golf Classic; Space Shuttle STS-77 Endeavour 11 lands; Chechnya signing peace treaty; 69th National Spelling Bee Wendy Guey spells "vivisepulture" correctly; Albert Belle using forearm to break up double play nearly breaks Brewers' 2nd baseman Fernando Vina's nose getting 2 game suspension; John Tesh's final day hosting "Entertainment Tonight"; Mark Van Thillo and Abigail Alling former biospherians win $100,000 lawsuit against Biospheric Development for Space Biospheres Ventures; Israel electing Benjamin Netanyahu

00

from *in-* "in" + *spirare* "to breathe"
p. part. of *inspirare* "inflame, blow into"

common knowledge

waiting for you as i
am and of nothing so will
you be as am i as
what would you be almost
my half of me
as it goes so it is
nothing and
it's real
when, much further on, you need auditors at
last must look things in the eye
one does not *need* an auditor

no matter. Always be
all ways kind to her
who shall be
cause you will a mother
be your mother too be
kind to me
the obligation

's gift to endure a
obligation's a gift
which mostly we'll learn just to

give you just so we must
listen you
common, all may resent you
when, one day yet, and out of nowhere waiting
for a bird to fly by
you may find yourself next to yourself a
waiting waiting there, someone too.

11.i MTV Movie Awards; Sony won't renew lease on megatron Times Square; 50th Tony Awards "Master Class"

and "Rent"; 51st U.S. Women's Open Golf Championship Annika Sorenstam; 9th Children's Miracle Network Telethon; Howard Stern Radio Show premieres Memphis Tennessee WMFS 92.9 FM; China agreeing to world ban on atomic testing; Julia and Noah wed "All My Children"; 128th Belmont Rene Douglas aboard Editor's Note 2:28.96; 66th French Women's Tennis Steffi Graf beats A. S. Vicario 63 67 108; Dean Jones career-best 5-112 for Derbyshire vs. Hampshire; Lloyd and Titchard complete 358 for 4th wicket Lancs vs. Essex; PBA National Championship Butch Soper; 66th French Men's Tennis Yevgeny Kafelnikov beats M. Stich 76 75 76; Michelle McGann LPGA Oldsmobile Golf Classic; Sunday League game Kent 6-314 overhaul Leicestershire's 4-311; 30th Music City News Country Awards Alan Jackson; Colorado Avalanche sweep Florida Panthers winning 1-0 in 6 periods; Howard Stern Radio Show premieres Toledo Ohio WBUZ 106.5 FM; Intel releasing 200 mhz pentium chip; Stanley Cup Colorado Avalanche sweep Florida Panthers in 4 games; Bob Dole Senator-R-Kansas resigning from U.S. senate to run for president; 3 Philadelphia Federal Court judges overturning U.S. indecency ban on internet; Montana Freemen giving up to FBI after 81 days; "Cable Guy" Jim Carrey released; Balkan leaders signing accord on arms limits; Ella Fitzgerald dies; Karl Krikken out handled the ball for Derbyshire vs. Indians; 1st competitive game played on turf in Holland by third graders; 50th NBA Championship Chicago Bulls beat Seattle Supersonics 6 games; 96th U.S. Golf Open Steve Jones 278 Oakland Hills Country Club; Liselotte Neumann First Bank Edina Realty LPGA Golf Classic; Howard Stern Radio Show premieres Syracuse New York WAQX 95.7 FM; Space Shuttle STS-78 Columbia 20 launches; 29th Curtis Cup Great Britain and Ireland 11-6; Michael Moorer beats Axel Shultz in 11 IBF heavyweight fight; Saurav Ganguly 131 Lord's on Test cricket debut; Dottie Pepper LPGA Rochester International Golf Tournament; Nintendo 64 on sale Japan; "Tartuffe: Born Again" closes Circle in Square New York City 29 performances; truck bomb killing 19 U.S. base Saudi Arabia; China performs nuclear test Lop Nor PRC; "Nutty Professor" Eddie Murphy opens in theaters USA; Andrea Leah Plummer Tennessee 39th America's Junior Miss; Superman's Action Comic #1 from 1938 selling at Sotheby $61,900; "Buried Child" closes Brook Atkinson Theater New York City 77 performances; Caroline Frolic Miss Ontario crowned Miss Renaissance U.S.A.; Dottie Pepper ShopRite LPGA Golf Classic; "Moon Over Buffalo" closes Martin Beck Theater New York City 308 performances; "State Fair" closes Music Box Theater New York City 118 performances

He is a slow reader, prone to rolling her too many cigarettes, and nausea from coffee. His studies, which begin in any earnest way in anthropology, are slow to coalesce. He chooses what seemed necessary at the time, despite himself, but without enough sense turned to how this "necessity" had come to be. So what he learned to do as his reader is this: still with her cigarettes: to utilize any and all he in fact comes across, to read each as historically marked, a foot her glory, as always touching politically, the only reliable spheres in which a human body may be said to share his allotted time. This too was the only way by which he might have understood such terms as "allotment." He has rather little context in which to attempt this, not the requisite grasp and, therefore, control of cause and effect, to work against his, or her, otherwise unnoteworthy talents, which may or may not ever have taken place. Cause and effect. The tangible mandate of the atheism, which she seems to him to promise somewhat, intuitively sensible in today's cities, and which in its way would become peculiar, a late (finally) herald of the past, which still needed ███████ has enabled the obstacle of the failure in their romance to succeed, to the tune of a small tax on the organs.

the philosophy that promised to abstract the hopes
out of his feelings to be fixed henceforth

iii obstinate cultivators of earthly things had

i a hundred mouths

forever in a purer ▮▮▮▮

found ready welcome

9/11 2004 if I die while I'm sippin tea
don't even bother buryin me, returned she still lives but's a window
from a window, Port Authority, he says he needs chicken you know who
no longer knows him

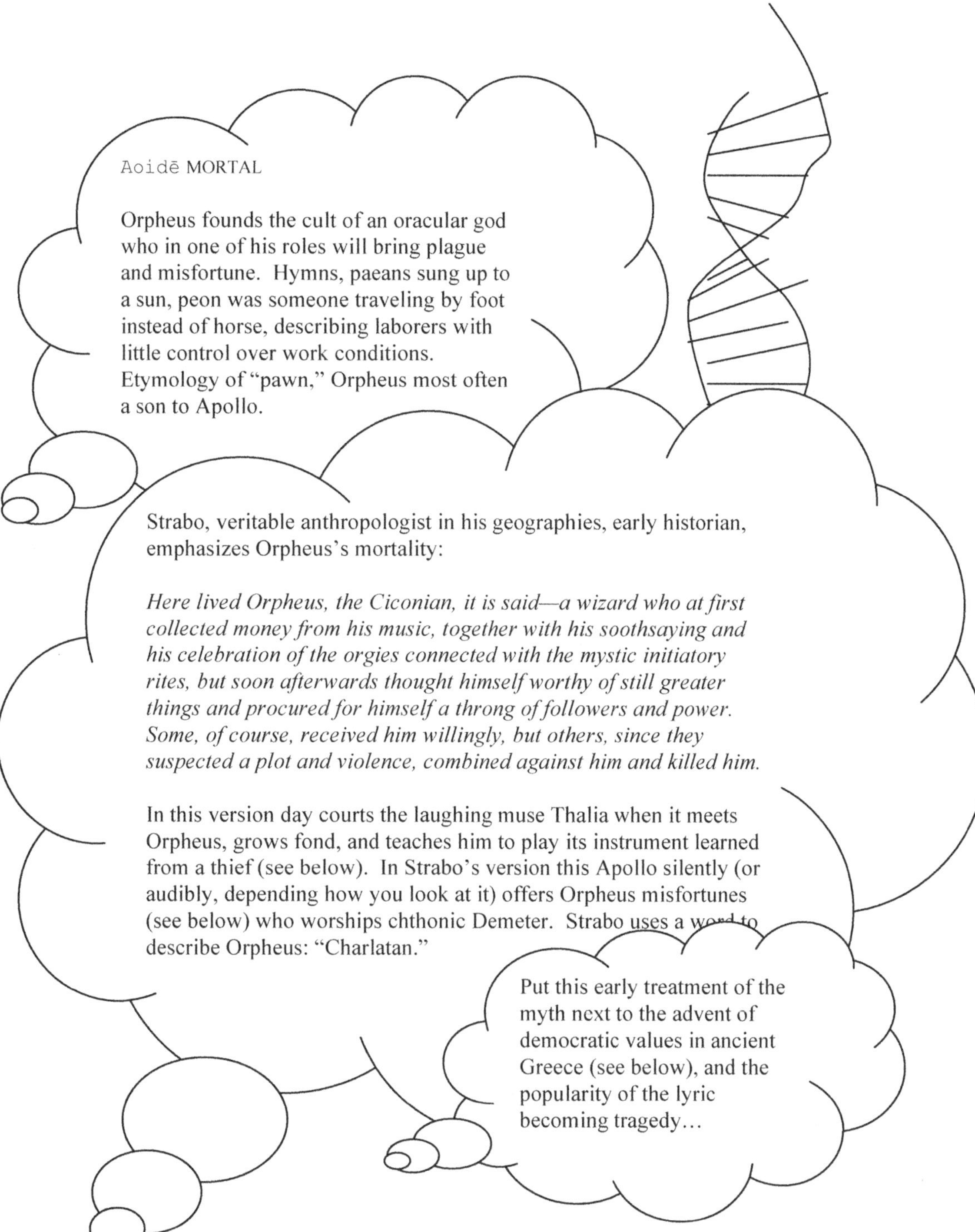

In versions prior to Virgil, in return for his beautiful music, the
"infernal gods" offer Orpheus mere apparitions of Eurydice.
He is punished for his cowardice, for resisting the death that
would actually return his dead mate—which is to say, his
personal muse, and a suspicious one you should remember,
appearing only at its disappearance, with Orpheus's own loss,
the one to whom his sad, most famous music is played.
Leading the gift he re-enters the living world and *looks* and his
apparition vanishes, the trick exposed, and he learns "what"
was gone shall be kept so. In some versions he is then the first
to name the light of day Apollo (thus he "founds Apollo's
cult") and, one morning, as he climbs the mountain to worship,
neglecting ablutions to his patron Dionysus, and the Maenads
tear him apart, he receives his second, final earthly reward.

Who or what ruins lyrical Orpheus,
conspires against him? Why must he
himself, eventually, by the time of
Virgil, Empire's poet, ruin the chance
of his dead, born(e) muse's, *actual*
return to the flesh on earth? Why, how,
does tragedy appropriate the lyric?

Strabo's homophonic "lyre / liar"…

Meletē IMMORTAL

The sun is also the divinity of
healing—of its lyre, of battle and
victory—Roman soldiers sung
paeans on the march. Thanks to
someone like Orpheus, Rome knew
Apollo.

Aeschylus identifies Gaia with Maia, Hermes's ma—and a
usual Zeus, his absent father. Guide to the underworld,
messenger of Olympus, Hermes is a bridge, between
divinities and men, master of the lyre. "Hermeneutics," the
art of interpreting hidden meanings, Hermes, born before
Dionysus, inventing a fire to parallel (see below)
Prometheus, who in Aeschylus, visits him on the
mountainside with a message—where matter-of-factly,
smugly, the patron of thieves urges a gutted and tragic
friend of man to repent of his allegiance and theft. Hermes,
trickster god of boundaries, "guide" to those already
removed (like Orpheus Prometheus).

The night of his first day he'd already slip away
to steal his elder half-brother's immortal herd of
cattle. He'll select two ("Hermes Logios"
Plato's god of persuasion) for slaughter,
dividing each into six portions—eleven
corresponding to the number of Olympians,
nixing the twelfth the remainder set beside
himself. The transgression, the work of this
eternal thief, will establish a new Apollonian
sacrifice among brotherhoods of men (and see
below). He'll hide the rest of the herd in a cave
and cover his tracks.

"nix" [31]

---

[31] A water sprite, usually in human form, or half-human half-fish. German, like the author's
father.

Once the sun has returned to its field, expecting to
find its cattle grazing, it uncovers the truth. It goes
to Maia in her cave (Gaia?) who defends her son's
innocence ("Orpheus worships chthonic Demeter"),
but Zeus intervenes, siding with enlightened day
(tyrannical dad, son-of-a-bitch). Hermes, from the
cradle of a cave predicting he'll be found out, has
killed a tortoise and strung its shell. In the midst of
arguing Hermes plucks the tune from the hollow
pleases his accuser—he will be granted the herd in
exchange for a wonderful instrument. For his
apparent gift, Hermes will now be kept busy, raised
to his Olympian errands' career. Later this half-
brother will trade his caduceus for Hermes's flu

Some of Hermes's offspring, all chimeric and related
to fertility: Pan, Hermaphroditus, Eros, Priapus,
Fortuna and the prince of thieves, Lone Wolf
Autolycus, "who makes his thefts as invisible as
possible." By breaking with tradition, authority, law
whatever, taboo, where lies, eloquence, seduction and
abduction are involved, and his hollow cavity's shell,
echoing, a new bond between divinity and men
appears. His promotion to a regime post whose
nature—yet the "immortal" herd receives such a
shepherd. This new peon (winged *feet*), functionary,
assimilate Olympian, bound herder's boredom to the
sky, across the invoking lips of men, a new "paean."
Kleos, rock, corporate, in need of its poet.

Homophonic lyre / liar, like "lute" and "loot," how it finds a mortal's hands—the sun, Delphic bringer of plague or healing, sometimes at once as the case may be, is the apparent medium—with his pythia—itself the unlikely thief of all that was Iris, caduceus, ladling "sleep" from the Styx, under us, closed eyelids, over those who perjure themselves—the locus of her heraldry and its knowledge will thus shift from the eye's closing to the ear's opening where day sticks and has rewarded, like Orpheus, Hermes' scheming. Put this development next to the flourishing of literary arts, the contest's performance in ancient Greece, the advent of its tragedies, states and decay, the spurning of epic, incorporation of lyric (1st Sappho) inventions of oratory and rhetoric—masochistic—and Rome's embrace of so much Greek.

It's not possible to flesh out all the details. Part of the problem and value of myth seems to lie in that it adapts. In *how* it adapts. E.g. slippage across Orpheus (like Prometheus), Hermes (like Iris) and Apollo, seemingly fosters awareness of true art or its melodious, generously selfish tongue which (Socratic) the west takes time to divorce, part and parcel to the advent of histories as verifiably disciplined—where song and the accounts of cheating immortality are once the literal history. "His stories." This garbled mind, of futurity, heralding itself in earth-borne garments, familiarly sociable terms, bodily doings, the anthropomorphizing of something otherwise felt as not, or Other—"genii"—*coins* the myth corresponds to your thoughts about today's truth not feeling good, nor meant to. Your poem, like Strabo suspicious, something like the Hermes of an Orpheus, wise and unwise and unwittingly easy Delphos, acoustics.

TELECOMMUNICATIONS IN THE VALLEY in the sand,
silica, pupil to "man's crown of distinction" [32]

p seeds of a thought

Relative to arsenic, "silicon"
then for the ███ add "sulfur"
"chlorine argon sodium abundance"
would have █████ not really, amassing
the "interstellar medium,"
the "iron peak" like a match struck
"chandrasekhar limit" some "degenerate matter
in its gas immersed, absorbing
neighbors in its collapse

q like solar flares

not collapsing "neutral" fluxes "incredibly high
there in the tube a rainbow's light until all light
line, "intake"

$p \supset q$

"there is no real
        real "stopping"
resistant some—like a worm's permit or a shell
a cheater'd cup—

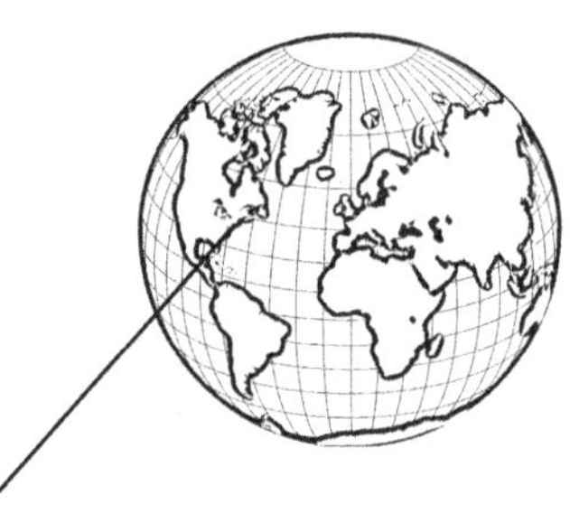

<hr>

[32] Mathematically, most of the cloaking constructions mentioned above have their origins in a singular transformation of space in which an infinitesimally small hole has been stretched to a ball (the boundary of which is the cloaking surface). An object can then be inserted inside the hole so created and made invisible to external observations. We call this process blowing up a point. The wormhole device has the effect of changing the topology of space and is theoretically described by means of an "invisibility coating." We conclude by describing other possible applications of wormhole devices, Patent Filing for Fractal Metamaterial Invisibility On-Off Cloak-On-Command.

a liar, Iris

water cups for water

under surface lurking humility

OF WELLS FAR GONE
early

ATTN:

mercurial discharge lamps like every tectonic shift persisting delivery past
obsolescence arrives its daughter stuffing envelopes pythia
and the slide, so badly it's
smudge perfect   lick glue, thick lipped

ATTN:

stamps the future   it's its tool it thirrrsts, mmmm
sure has grown   here is smart

ATTN:

good cause we do not much asking
decently now we're meeting—
whole ███ begun, existing—

ATTN:

with braised bodies walking briskly around heliotropic and only come worried
afluorescence, [33] cheapest light, clocks who fall out wage

---

[33] Background to US Patent 7470516 compositions and methods for cDNA synthesis: One of the most widely used techniques to study gene expression exploited first-strand cDNA for mRNA sequences as templates for amplification by the polymerase chain reaction, PCR. This method, often referred to as RNA PCR or reversetranscriptase PCR (RT-PCR), exploited the high sensitivity and specificity of the PCR process and was widely used for detection and quantification of RNA, until the ability to measure the kinetics of a PCR reaction by on-line detection in combination with RT-PCR techniques had enabled the accurate and precise measurement of RNA sequences with high sensitivity. This simpler, real-time, on-line approach to exploiting one of the most widely used techniques for studying gene expression utilized a double-strand specific fluorescent dye, ethidiumbromide, added to the amplification reaction of mRNA sequencing by PCR. The fluorescent signal generated at each cycle of PCR was proportional to the amount of PCR product. A plot of fluorescence versus cycle number was used to describe the kinetics of amplification, and an afluorescence threshold level was used to define a fractional cycle number related to initial template concentration. Specifically the log of the initial template concentration was inversely proportional to the fractional cycle number (threshold cycle, or Ct), defined as the intersection of the fluorescence versus cycle number curve with the fluorescence threshold. Higher amounts of starting template resulted in PCR detection at a lower Ct value, whereas lower amounts required a greater number of PCR cycles to achieve an equivalent fluorescent threshold (Ct) and were detected at higher Ct values. Typically the setting of this fluorescence threshold was defined as a level that represented a statistically significant increase over background fluorescentnoise. Since this would

freeze   sync again, manageable

will no matter   be smooth a little matter
thinking i hope not within what's being made which

                                        has been making ATTN:

will keeps it up   tries be hard   nearby board's enforceable safeguard
-er thinking   but the smudge so much more
                                        the stick couldn't think—

ATTN: SOCIA (f. SOCIUS) Latin for partner, companion, associate from SOCIETAS
fellowship implying union for a common purpose, no mere assembly ███████████████
███—ugly as sin. Once held to her breast, miraculous thing:

Light gives light to the discoverer—
ad infinitum.   April 10, A. D., 1818

To all the world——I declare the earth is hollow and habitable within; containing
a number of solid concentric spheres, one within the other, and that it is open
at the poles ██ or ██ degrees. I pledge my life in support of this truth, and am
ready to explore the hollow, if the world will support and aid me in this
undertaking.

██████████ late captain of infantry.

N. B. ——I have ready for the press a treatise on the principles of matter,
wherein I show proofs of the above positions, account for various phenomena and
discuss ████████████████████████

                His Terms Were Easy.

---

occur at an early stage in the PCR process when critical substrates were not limiting,
quantification of starting templates occurred over a broad dynamic range with high
accuracy, precision, and sensitivity. A major problem in the understanding of gene
expression patterns for gene discovery and identification of metabolic pathways was the
limitations of contemporary methods for accurate quantification. Use of real-time PCR
methods provided a significant improvement towards this goal. However, real-time PCR
quantification of mRNA is still bounded by limitations of the process of reverse
transcription.

My terms are the patronage of this and the new worlds.

I dedicate to ▮▮▮▮▮▮▮▮▮▮▮▮▮▮▮▮▮▮ I select ▮▮▮▮▮▮▮▮▮▮▮▮▮▮▮▮▮▮ as my protectors.

I ask 100 brave companions, well equipped, to start from ▮▮▮▮ in the fall season, with reindeer and sleighs, on the ice of the frozen sea. I engage we find a warm and rich land, stocked with thrifty vegetables and animals, if not ▮▮ on reaching one degree northward of latitude ▮▮ whence we will return in the succeeding spring.

▮▮▮

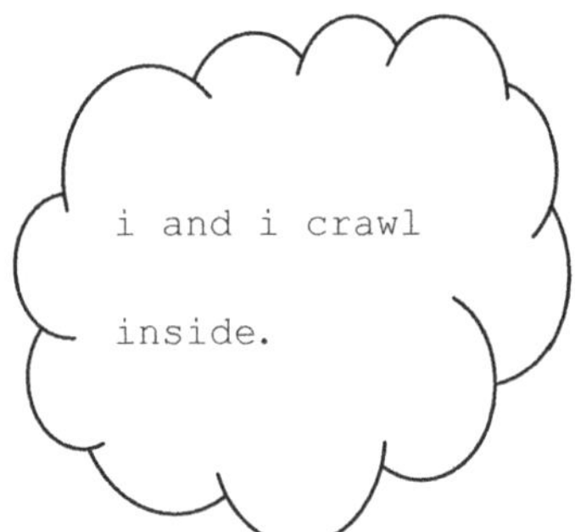

pythia storms and travel and rabbit
ears swiveled the 21st century

down ██████ dumb
dog's head cocking's a little more uncertain
than all the news put
together Brookhaven's
atomic

████ so today's the beef
grown cheaper than the hometown

was subsidized Arabian horses, mounted whistles, uniform
illegible tags kept milking
is your city or avenue incunabular balloons,
mark the year for indelible banners
some passing peacefully

abreast, the stopper flaunts
        permit, after the photograph [34]

me, and apparently some others
        still ████ to

look to wondering face
portholes of the plane
cargo subscriptions, wondering
red drapings orderly

tags given nothing
linguistic so if one were to affect it
symmetries redundant of bodies, generative
erasures, I imagine

---

[34] "Passengers aboard the commercial flight bringing home the body of 2nd Lt. Jim Cathey watch as his casket is unloaded by a Marine honor guard at Reno-Tahoe International Airport," from "Final Salute," Rocky Mountain News, 11/11 2005. This story wins him, whom their wives, probably lonely, invite in, the Pulitzer Prize for "feature writing."

you come with some papers
a knock and it's permanent,
(theoretical and sound)

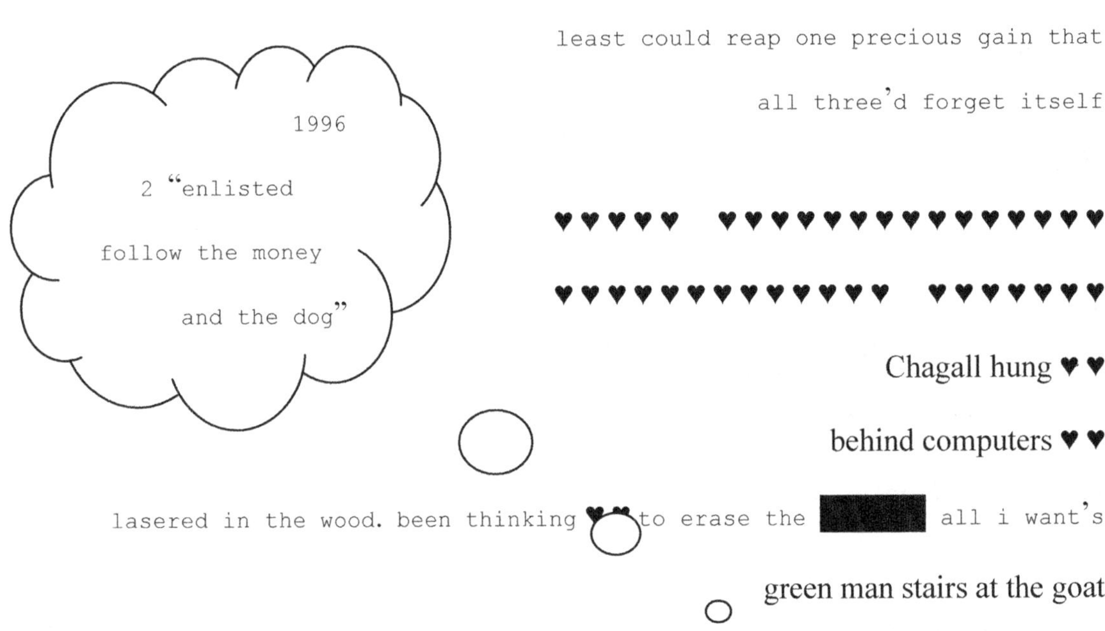

like the prodigy whose love is here at

least could reap one precious gain that

all three'd forget itself

Chagall hung ♥ ♥

behind computers ♥ ♥

lasered in the wood. been thinking to erase the all i want's

green man stairs at the goat

future coffee [35]

returning from seeing your own birthplace to distant home you must

have taken pictures i'd sure love to see them hung in our

hallways like

nickels on tongues the mind

in our belly turns and for the fire in the mind my

toes

☼

POSSIBILITY AND THE VILLAGE

here goes again—green
men stare at the goat
fluid line—him bearing the sprig
milk made in its head
their eyes meet once
tool—scratched it through the paint

    whole zero
—what
are you doing with my belt o
honey's coming through so
water's
on the moon's news
may we live—down there.

---

[35] ♀ an early poem he will write on coffee but nowhere
now—he'll have to kill him.

that was the peak

that was intended to be the peak

so tomorrow

the whole ██████   seats with the gravy plus

                                                                       oracles ▲

                                                               trembling at the deep

                                                             experiment's wakened a

frontispiece two-page tinctured spread in bursting sun moon unconstellated stars and Uranus and what looks to be 2 bombers in cargo that forms the canopy over the bullet train position of the river curving toward you in a trough from under the bridged and banked distance's silver metropolis of the future on the one hand a coalstack factory like a city lit well on the other foremost a furrowed hair family unit in togas whose mother looks intelligent like ████████████ but bigger eyes sitting and reading to the industriously pleasant looking daughter who sits lace on her hands locks the elbows and perhaps too her comic magazine son who probably has organized disorganized baseball fixates on his own smaller book while a muscle of the father yet graceful without even his club membership probably his job is hard to determine stands reading the largest himself behind all of them his probably remarkable pages remembered with ornate ropes lick your finger a huge angel of flowing robes wearing its androgynous bowl cut with feathers appears poised to plant a crown of ribbon and laurel on his head

FBI agent charged with spying for Moscow; "Hughie" closes at Circle in Square Theater New York City; 26th New York City Women's Marathon Anuta Catuna Romania 2:28:18; 27th New York City Marathon Giacomo Leone Italy 2:09:54; "It's a Slippery Slope" opens Vivian Beaumont Theater New York City; Mayumi Hirase wins LPGA; Toray Japan Queens Cup; Yankees shortstop Derek Jeter unanimous choice AL Rookie of the Year; Clinton-Gore ticket winning national election; Republicans retaining control of Congress; Los Angeles Dodger Todd Hollandsworth NL Rookie of Year; Defense Advanced Research Projects Agency (DARPA) announcing Teledyne Ryan Aeronautical Systems gets $24,381,746 cost-plus-award-fee contract for Miniature Air-Launched Decoy Advanced Concept Technology Demonstration; "3 Sisters" opens Lunt-Fontanne Theater New York City; NFL/Heisman Trophy Winner Mike Rozier shot several times; Wasim Jaffer 314 2nd cricket FC game Mumbai vs. Saurashtra; Braves John Smoltz NL Cy Young Award; Mid-air collision India kills 342; Toronto's Pat Hentgen AL Cy Young Award; Padres third baseman Ken Caminiti 4th unanimous winner NL MVP; UNSCOM unable to determine full extent of Iraq's weapons program; "Three Sisters" closes Lunt-Fontanne Theater New York City; "Chicago" opens Richard Rodgers Theater New York City; Texas Ranger Juan Gonzalez AL MVP; Texaco settling racial bias suit; "Into the Whirlwind" opens Lunt-Fontanne Theater New York City; Hutu refugees returning to Rwanda; 18th ACE Cable Awards HBO 28 awards; "Into the Whirlwind" closes Lunt-Fontanne Theater New York City 2 performances; "Present Laughter" opens Walter Kerr Theater New York City; Sam's Town Bowling Invitational; Eappens hire nanny Louise Woodward later charged with murder; Albert Belle signing five-year $55 million White Sox; "God Said Ha!" opens Lyceum Theater New York City 22 performances; 1st Strategic Force annual war games; "Sex and Longing" closes Cort Theater New York City; Space Shuttle STS-80 Columbia 21 launches; "Rehearsal" opens Criterion Theater New York City; O. J. Simpson taking stand as hostile witness in wrongful death suit saying it is absolutely not true; Irebe Skliva 18 Greece 46th Miss World; CFL Grey Cup Toronto beats Edmonton 43-37 Hamilton Ontario; "Juan Darien - A Carnival Mass" opens Vivian Beaumont Theater New York City; rookie Karrie Webb ITT LPGA Tour Championship; former KGB officer Vladimir Galkin clear of espionage charges; Mashonaland defeats Matabeleland Logan Cricket Cup; Mohammad Wasim 109 Test cricket debut Pakistan vs. New Zealand Lahore; after 24 years Disneyland Main Street Electrical Parade ending; international assistance to emerging democracies increasing significantly; runaway housing prices should moderate in 1997; baseball owners still approving inter-league play; Colbert Floyd and Irwin Wendy's Senior 3 Tour Golf Challenge; Davies Sheehan and Sorenstam Wendy's Lady's 3 Tour Golf; Love and Stewart Wendy's Men's 3 Tour Golf Challenge

♥ ♥ ♥ ♥ ♥　♥ ♥ ♥ ♥ ♥ ♥ ♥ ♥ ♥ ♥ ♥ ♥ ♥ ♥

♥ ♥ ♥ ♥ ♥ ♥ ♥ ♥ ♥ ♥ ♥ ♥　♥ ♥ ♥ ♥ ♥ ♥

mighty vision the worker of our earlier ♥ ♥
♥

age broadening the highway over ♥ ♥

bridges dimples pounds in the ♥

transformable vehicle
your wrapping paper lied
once chimney over porches
snowball stacks
in forts salt
wreak havoc on the roads
driveways appear and dis appear
and planet big sheets of ice
and late as usual hope arrives
comprehensible as ever
zero's little you
forget how rambunctious we are

THE STORY WAS THIS OTHER ONE

2001 THE MAN ON THE DUMP

because i will not end with that, rolling against the breeze, past the actual [36]
fort trampled chain link
down to wash

in sands some SHIELD and access its breakwater foundations made
for sturdy lounging impressed
not love, bored

the sun in the stone, pits dimple the cannon, register
with gull shits
Ascent shunt
look out boats ! school

---

[36] "commodities." as if ever his side the fence.

"something meandered
into a lake. eras

"patched rock the peering walls
closed.

"cannon hole. breakwater
fell away.

"fossil. steel mesh. where the grass ended a trampled
fence, like paths down.

The myth-pattern that does emerge from ███████ can be seen as the result of a
simple interaction between a frontiersman and his environment——the end product,
not of a bardic, myth-making consciousness, but of ███████ letting his words and
thoughts shape themselves to the events of the hunt, whose narrative is in
itself an implicit argument for an heroic theory of history, but █████ is not
interested in achieving the critical distance from his tale that would enable
him to generalize broadly. This turn toward the █████ ultimately liberated the
myth-making mind of the ███████ and awakened them to at least a partial
awareness of their own special psychology. The ███████ viewed the █████ as
projections of the ████ within themselves, as well as the agent of an external
malice——a vision whose paradox is fruitful ground for a wide range of
imaginative speculation on the nature of reality and of history and on the
possible roles and powers men can assume in the world.

85th Davis Cup France beats Sweden Malmo 3-2; Lance Klusener takes 8-64 in debut Test cricket trouncing India; 7th Billboard Music Awards; 1st Mars rover launching Cape Canaveral; Orlando Magic tying NBA record fewest points scored since inception of 24-second clock losing to Cleveland 84-57; Madeleine Albright appointed 1st female U.S. secretary of state; "Dreams and Nightmares" opens Martin Beck Theater New York City; Players' Union approving new collective bargaining agreement; Portland's Jermaine O'Neal 18 youngest NBA player; Mashonaland defeats England 1st class tour match; Space Shuttle STS-80 Columbia 21 lands; Donna Andrews Mike Hulbert LPGA J C Penney Golf Classic; "God Said Ha!" closes Lyceum Theater New York City 22 performances; assassination attempt on Uday Hussain; Marlins signing 6th free agent since November 22 Moises Alou; Kofi Annan UN secretary general; free agent Roger Clemens signing Toronto Blue Jays; 12th Soap Opera Digest Awards; 62nd Heisman Trophy Award Danny Wuerffel Florida quarterback; Dottie Pepper Juli Inkster LPGA Diner's Club Golf Matches; Jim Colbert Bob Murphy Diner's Club Senior PGA Golf Matches; Undersecretary of Defense for Acquisition and Technology approving revised DarkStar High Altitude Endurance Unmanned Aerial Vehicle program; Tom Lehman Duffy Waldoff Diner's Club PGA Golf Matches; 1st Test cricket match Zimbabwe vs. England; television industry executives adopting ratings system; FBI agent charged with spying for Moscow; Vladimir Galkin back in Russia; "Once Upon a Matress" opens Broadhurst New York City 187 performances; Pakistan all out 67 losing to Tasmania by an inning; Steelers' Kordell Stewart running quarterback record 80-yard TD; Wendy's Three Tour Golf Challenge; Zimbabwe and England draw Bulawayo Test cricket with England needing 1 to win; 4 women ordained priests Jamaica 330-year Anglican history; thousands marching Belgrade continuing protest against president's annulment of election results; Carquest Bowl 7 Miami beats Virginia 31-21; India all out for 66 at Durban making 100 in cricket 1st inning; "Dreams and Nightmares" closes Martin Beck Theater New York City; "Skylight" closes Royale Theater New York City; "Taking Sides" closes Atkinson Theater New York City

ring recorded

a spurt

every seventeen years. [37]
Near where we grew up another planet
hatching cicada morning   groping
up the trunk

bigger surge   by afternoon
on the planet
        hatching again
    wings in to

☼

    slug or totally clumsy
    dawn all   lain

                                    at

---

[37] In northeastern American woodlands a brood of periodical cicada nymphs hatch drop and burrow into the ground where for seventeen years they feed on sap from tree roots, passing through five molts. Then all at once in late spring they tunnel to the surface, largest migration of the planet, up into tree branches, where they take their sixth. Soon the woods' inhabitants are gorging themselves on these adults as they mate lay eggs and die. Their carcasses piled and decomposing, their eggs hatching and the cycle beginning again, "predator satiation." There are broods passing somewhere every year with trees recording inordinate growth.

sundown

Fits and starts mine in the room, all through a house
Lack, desired, outside the window
mine come from dirt
voluminous shelf
even as we hope its
Influxed desires complicates "yard" as
We we'd sit in its house, in my office, my room
overlap
like cells no
something else

2006

ALARM'S GLOSS AND THE SORRY NOTE
(ten covered there it's named outskirts of town, card to punch)

sun

/ CHANTER

CHANTER

☼

CHANTER

GRACKLES

DELPHI INC

outskirts of town morning treks
hope *serviced*   newspapered
                / a response at the entrance

☼♀:

(man.)

SUN

Socia (f. SOCIUS) – Latin – partner, companion,
associate. From SOCIETAS – fellowship –
implying union for a common purpose and
no mere assembly

OPPORTUNITY UNLIMITED and many manuals [38]
kleos compositions for two

easy to mistake our talent everywhere
specifically, here and there, the sober delay
depending upon you

while some medicine warped
organ's prescribed
sobriety slips of

paper over
functioning madness
a power to reason

! like land's ration. the directions in that place
the mail box was barely
proper signed

for elation the van's
a nude fear
! shiny package all the way around

who sidled
its fork
to lift actually

work made by button
securest box, secure in our vista where our genius says
genius from the van

from news exposed ▮▮▮▮▮▮ on cameras it's not deemed
public and what's finally given !
them to you your signature does
their work

to memorize a new pre-script re-read

---

[38] As we pronounce them, doing them much wrong, have been to me more bountiful than hope,
less timid than desire.

is logged, constant line yes
a wording flows
! and harvests to create once clearly

meaning definably you'll give her permissions
and her allowance
let the old dwarf stutter
▮▮▮▮▮ has banned her

obesity issues
anyway, at this point the persona must understand that it is on the schedule glistening
lists' firm public

relations though to her peepholes'
stutter

grid in the ceiling's black orb above
all glistening spittle never mind
spread sheets let this dwarf stutter ! this man
needs new shorts ! we leak

you must watch your figure wear her face abuse
something planted with loved ones

FABLE

April 1, 2009
Offices of Legal Counsel
Contest Oversight Committee
National Poetry Council

Memorandum for ███████ wise Mouth for the National Endowment

Pure poetry is conversant with an imaginary world, peopled with beings of its own creation. It deals in splendid imagery, bold fiction, and allegorical personages. It is necessarily obscure to a certain degree; because, having to do with images generated within the mind, it cannot be at all comprehended by any whose intellect has not been exercised in similar contemplations; while the conceptions of the poet (often highly metaphysical) are rendered still more remote from common apprehension by the figurative in which they are clothed. The substratum, if I may so express myself, or subject matter, which every composition must have, is, in a poem of this kind, so extremely slender, that it requires not only art, but a certain artifice of construction, to work it up into [its] beautiful place. [39]

To that end we agree to conduct ourselves as ethically as possible, addressing any unethical behavior defining conflict of interest for all parties involved, to make the mechanics of our ███████ process available, so that each model can be run, to reinforce our integrity and dedication. [40]

> i.   Do I attempt to resolve the issue by bringing the behavior to the ███████ of colleagues?
>
> ii.   If the behavior appears to be due to lack of sensitivity, knowledge, or experience, are hard solutions really appropriate?
>
> iii.   A fire threatens the ██████ ; do we save a ████████ painting or a young woman who hadn't many years left anyhow?
>
> iv.   ██ is a strong conductor for doubts and fears. May we enter those green fields?

Suave regards,

---

[39] genius, 1756
[40] codes, condensed, 2005

Assistant to a Programs Coordinator

Memorandum for ████████ Acting Counsel to a National Poetry Council

You have `ab extra` asked for my Office's views on whether certain proposed conduct would not violate the prohibition against ████ as expressed by ████████████ ████████████ in their collectively bargained and recently ratified code of ethics. You have asked for this advice in the course of recent accusations `cf.` ████████████ that ████████████ are actively engaged in sponsoring ████████ while effectively debilitating future ████████████ noteworthy shapers of thought for several ████████ which ████ currently finds itself engaging in psychologically armed conflicts involving recent oral ████████████ and like last week's ████████████ as well as miscellaneous ████████████ `cf.` "The State of Poetry Today," enclosed and forthcoming in our Program Committee's annual Budget Report in ways that have ████ been fully determined. After review by my Office, this letter memorializes our previous oral advice given you most recently ████████████ that your proposed conduct would not violate the prohibition.

I

████████ pursuant to ████████ clearly in place in its ████████ position, has special ████ in contrast to the domestic realm, due to ████████ and ████████ over diplomatic relations. There can be little doubt that a matter that is fundamentally ████████ in nature implies the direction of the common ████ for directing and employing its common ████ forms, a usual and essential part in the definition of ████████ Thus earlier in this current conflict I concluded that ████ will be at its zenith under such operations, `cf.` ████████ where a reduced role in the efforts of the ████ over time and in similar circumstances, generally defer to ████████ concerning the conduct of construing generally applicable ████ so as not to apply to its own conduct during basic allocations of ████ As my office explained in rejecting the application which would have prohibited the seizure of vessels during the current previously concluded ████ `cf.` ████████ the absence of a clear ████████ ██ or context for its prohibition, suggested its intent to circumscribe this ████ Moreover I did not believe it should have been interpreted to impose such a restriction on the deference especially appropriate in the area of respect inherent to directing unto our general ████ construed as not applying. Pursuant to the conduct of ████ during any ████████ that regulate the ability to determine the treatment of serious ████ I do not believe any ████████ such as prohibitions against assault, maiming, or ███ stalking, pursuant to any express ███ would allow it to infringe on ███ over ███

II

In my view we may no more regulate the ability to detain than we may regulate the ability to direct movements. In fact general applicability belies any argument that ███ in any case should be applied to persons, under the direction of ███ for many years natural rights have hitherto supplied. [41] Such a canon's several highly illustrative contexts cannot be discussed in this memorandum, as the application of these to the conduct here considered would risk depriving the ███ of a recognized prerogative historically free. Treat ███ as you wish, this power has been vested in its clause ███ As one commentator has suggested, [42] we are more often than not treated as we are liable to be treated, so there is almost no ███ ███ respecting them, and thus no ███ is owed towards them or anything that cannot enjoy the privilege accorded its own gifts of nature. To demand we treat such ███ under any traditional practice, as expressed in the ███ must be left to the ███ discretion. As one commentator has stated, [43] the treatment must be left to the discretion of the threatened. While ███ efforts frequently require the literal violation of facially applicable ███ as we indicate above, and which we develop below, to persons acting under the color of ███ indicates no intent to apply this to conduct or personnel.

III

Certain acts will however consistently reappear in cases pertinent to yours or are of such a barbaric nature that it is likely ███ would find that allegations here I do not consider the reliability of intelligence produced of such treatment as severe beatings, using instruments such as iron barks, truncheons, and clubs, threats of imminence such as mock executions, removing extremities, burning, especially burning with cigarettes, electric shocks to genitalia, or threats to do so, rape or sexual assault, or injury to an individual's sexual organs, or threatening to do any of these sorts of acts, forcing others to watch, would, though one cannot say with certainty, falling short of these, not miss ███ I do believe that the actual ███ would have had to have been similar to ███ in its extreme nature, and in the type of harm caused to violate the ███ or any functioning ███ Furthermore ███ would hold the

---

[41] Uncle Sigmund's brought to the Pythia.

[42] ███ is used because the discourse that follows is critical as well as fictitious; ███ is used in the sense that it is essential in the formulation of a discourse; ███ because the writing of a discourse always implies bringing together pieces of other discourses; an unfinished endless discourse because what is ███ here is open at both ends, and as such more could be added endlessly

[43] "The totally blasted landscape is a really hard place to leave someone."

██████ subject to jurisdiction in only two contexts. For your purposes the act may fall under the jurisdiction of crimes committed against humanity only if committed as part of a widespread and systematic ████ directed against ██████ while the ████████████ suggests that the relevant entity cannot grow ██████ prior to itself, so must therefore not be definably restricted, nor ever directly related really, but widely constituted as something dispersed around the ██████ technically, rather than bound to any state.

IV

Indeed as I explain in discussing the prerogative of the ██████████ it is well established that the ██████████ does retain the discretion to act as it sees fit, so long as the method does not ████████████████████████████████ This type of assault has, expanding upon III, not been committed. Even in the event of a more direct physical contact, as I understand the situation, something less concrete would have had to have been established, having been insufficient to demonstrate that the type of method involving alterations to its environment has proven problematic cf. ████████████ pursuant to ████████████ not only because no visibly ████████████ had been used, but also because such alterations were so unlikely to involve the necessary intent to inflict bodily injury, as the method under contemplation has not involved the acts enumerated, Webster's New International Dictionary. The ██████ will not fall within the purview of this because ████████ requires specific intent to maim, disfigure, so the absence of such intent is a complete defense to a charge of maiming. Thus even if severe pain did knowingly result from ██████ if causing such harm was not the ultimate objective, it has lacked the requisite intent, though not the infliction of pain or suffering, here a step well removed from the kind that would be equivalent to the pain that would be associated with serious physical injury resulting in a loss of significant body function, which would likely have resulted if that pain or suffering was from one of the ██████ not advocated by ██ ████ In addition its ████ must cause long-term ██████ harm. Indeed this view of the act is consistent with ████████ common meaning, generally understood to involve intense or excruciating pain, or put another way, extreme anguish, WNID. In short, reading your proposition as a whole, it is plain that ████████ would encompass only ████████████ as the purpose of the analysis here would be to ascertain what could cross the threshold of producing the list of illustrative purposes for which it is inflicted.

Please let us know if we may be of further assistance.

Acting Counsel

NOTE FROM THE TEXT—the borders between quote and misquote, fragment and whole, human and not, trauma and elation, love and ethic, invention and accuracy, too uncertain for unraveling. [44]

THEREFORE, IN LINE WITH YOUR GENERAL PROBLEM:

Ecocriticism, Ecopoetics, Legibility: Among Other Things, the Objectively Signified

Philosophical skepticism aims to demonstrate that our attempts to make unequivocally valid claims about the world are ultimately misguided. To put it simply, he sought to show that the history of Western thought tried and failed to nail down the essences of things because things do not have essences to speak of. A subtle dialectician, he argued that there was nothing as unstable as the notion of a stable identity and nothing less knowable than what appears directly before us, DK

There is no longer any credible way of theorizing interiority as a pastoral refuge from the annihilations of culture, DC

Words are only frames you will hardly know who I am or what I mean no comfortable conclusion but I shall be good health to nevertheless letters are scrawls turnabouts astonishments strokes cuts masks filter and fibre your blood, SH / WW[w]

belief since the 1990s a growing field has concerned itself with the interactions between literature and environment. More than nature writing, ecocriticism "takes its energy not from a central methodological paradigm of inquiry but from a pluriform commitment to the urgency of rehabilitating that which has been effectively marginalized by mainstream societal assumptions." [1] The literary theorist, naturalist included, historically concerns itself with the relationships between writers and texts and their social, cultural, economic, political, readerly, human contexts. Ecocriticism distinguishes itself by factoring into the

---

[44] There. Named.

conversation a text's relationship to, and engagements with, recognizably inhuman spaces.

I begin with this basic introduction to an already vibrant field of inquiry because at its root, when emphasizing the "nonhuman" and our relationship to it, the value of an ecocritical writing practice harmonizing with constructivist realities might be overlooked. Can we think, and therefore write, about nonhuman environments beyond their human-centered productions while admitting that the same inevitably shape and inform our engagements with the places where we are? Specifically, how to consider human imaginations from an ecocritical point of view? If we treat this imagination as simultaneously "socialized" and "natural" phenomena—as physiological process that eco-logically can and can't be understood beyond the supply of human needs and desires, that will not be escaped as we are possessed of its logic—will we find ourselves in a position to accurately and beneficially explore texts' functions or potential? Constructivist approaches to nature as "discursive strategy" [2] argue it's an idea specific to time and place, a rhetorical concept serving practical human purposes. The ecocritic sees this opportunity to distinguish between abstract categories of thought and material, nonhuman environments in which they occur. [3] What would an ecocritical poetic that not only admits and confronts but also embraces and *indulges* psychological, cultural, politicized, even received representations and misrepresentations of nature look like? Could such a thing qualify as "ecocritical?" I argue that an ecopoetic indulging constructivist theory is worthwhile, reflexively realizing the human and nonhuman as independent while mutual states. By looking at two poems written prior to contemporary ecocriticism, I also mean to suggest that poets have for some time been interested in the text's possibility, point and difficulty regarding nonhuman phenomena.

Jonathan Levin acknowledges "the affinity between language and sociopolitical environment":

Almost no one still defends the belief that language or discourse is a "hermetic" concern: the consensus position is much more properly regarded as one that holds that language and discourse shape our social and (for some) physical environments. This is a social constructionist position, and in its most radical forms…it might even be held to imply an exceedingly attenuated commitment to the reality of the external world, but it is not a narrowly formalist position. [4]

He argues, "language at once enables and limits our recognition" of facts, but has trouble with the notion of a purely "referential world." [5] Nonetheless, in his reading of Maurice Merleau-Ponty, he insists we must "recognize that prereflective, primordial experience, which all humans undergo, is…quite difficult (if not impossible) to conceptualize, because our concepts belong to a language that systematically disregards and devalues it": [6]

Yet, there is a world of silence, the perceived world. There is an order where there are non-linguistic significations—yes, non-linguistic significations, but they are not accordingly positive…this silence will not be the contrary of language. [7]

Recognizing one's *linguistic condition* he calls for a "phenomenological ecopoetics" [8] whose product is "the verbal record of an interactive encounter in the world of our sensory experience between the human psyche and nature, where nature retains its autonomy." [9] Literature is seen here as an opportunity for "authentic" experience of "material place." [10] If an "interactive encounter" with "autonomous" nature, an idea that would "enable and limit our recognition" of the fact (why not dependent nature?), could in all its difficulty be recorded, then language becomes a site for authentic encounters with things inhuman. According to Levin, with language we do form what is beyond our ability to speak, bring into light a word's embeddedness, power and vulnerability.

It is this self-referential aspect of language that must complicate any word approaching "autonomy." Harriet Tarlo describes the constructivist project: "[It has] persisted in drawing our attention to the gap between language and, (by extension, literature) and the world." [11] Bakhtin is here: "Actual social life and historical becoming create within an abstractly unitary national language a multitude of concrete worlds, a multitude of bounded verbal ideological and social belief systems." [12] Unique historical periods and ideological contexts produce the differential, referential vectors of our words: "Each word tastes of the context and contexts in which it has lived its socially charged life; all forms are populated by intentions." [13] Bakhtin deems shared language "heteroglot opinion" [14] reflecting site-specific values within human networks and communities. [15] The very chance for speech is to always already have evoked, indulged, and legitimated a familiar paradigm. All utterance is already suspiciously propped up, dependent, questionable.

But neither are the chances of successfully conversing with the nonhuman (however absurd the attempt *may* seem) helped by post-structural de-constructions. When Derrida argues the signifier can only be approached in terms of what it does not signify, absence constitutes signification and by extension, conceptual presence:

> ...the signified concept is never present in itself, in an adequate presence that would refer only to itself. Every concept is necessarily and essentially inscribed in a [linguistic] chain or a system [of signifiers], within which it refers to another and to other concepts, by the systematic play of differences. Such a play, then—différance—is no longer simply a concept, but the *possibility of conceptuality,* of the conceptual system and process in general. [16]

As our words and thoughts acquire significance and reference by terms they will not refer to, the signified, as the chance we'll know *anything,* can exist only as potential through their "systematic play of differences." Perpetual deferral of selfhoods, through conditional presences, each idea lags in this gainful, chance-based system of its loss. [17] Where consciousness is not possible prior to speech or its signs, [18] these negations of voices, words and texts imply conceivable environments whose foundation is substantive *nothing,* the "inapparent relation between two spectacles." [19] "It is a tomb" [20] with "no support to be found and no depth to be had for this bottomless chessboard where being is set in play," [21] a short jump to Baudrillard's hallucinatory "generation by models of a real without origin or reality." [22]

The idea that material environments cannot be understood beyond socialized conceptual frames seems truthful, accurate, believable, useful—as do notions that language actually can or does form from while giving form to things beyond, or within, those frames. Our understanding of the gaps between signifiers and signifieds begins in asking how effective language comes to be—by a life, by lives, discourses, times and things, by itself—which includes another question, what is language for—before determining success, failure, potential. The question is not new, nor trivial; by indulging the simultaneity of human (signifier) and nonhuman (among other things, the objectively signified) realities and environments under the fraught banner of "place," an ecocritically constructivist approach to text and production engenders ontological and phenomenal dilemmas in which the chance of realizing, possibly understanding, what we and the other *actually are* is at stake.

According to Michael Cohen, the problem is one of "wilderness versus the city, nature versus nurture: these dualities are constantly breaking down and yet are surprisingly eternal in our discourse." [23] Recognizing this, some critics have prioritized the felt experience of lived spaces. [24] In "Cultural Geography and the Place of the Literary," Sara Blair writes:

> Over the last two decades [printed in 1998], a constellation of texts and
> scholars...has not only declared that history as god-term is dead, but that

temporality as the organizing form of experience has been superseded by spatiality, the affective and social experience of space. [25]

"Historically sedimented sites" are now seen as the "built environment" of late-stage capitalism where "all that is solid has melted into air…conceptual maps predicated on clear distinctions between outside and inside, public and private, authentic and themed, become ever less relevant." [26] Environments are best understood as "felt performance" [27] or "lived structures of feeling." [28] Here we are "symptomatic" of what we derive from and occupy, [29] dissolving into our surroundings (as) partially human, partially inhuman things—political, economic, climatic production—and as such embody shifting *versions* of places. Here being is variable, involved, legible *narration*.

Here, though contact with the nonhuman is tainted with the human vessel of the contact, the opposite is also true, that the human element is tainted with the inhuman aspect not only of the contacted, but also of (the) contact itself. As Blair contends, "referent and signifier in American discourses of nature have been mutually productive of one another." She understands the ethic that "redirect[s] our attention from 'how culture forms us' to 'what our culture is doing, quite tangibly, to our earth.'" [30] Even so, she maintains that drawing "a distinction between space or place as abstract category and 'authentic' material place…whose protection will redeem human beings…from their own waste and greed…remains profoundly problematic." [31] Blair mistrusts "mythologizing rhetorics of space and the nation…an evolving imaginative production of 'landscapes lost' and 'paradise paved.'" [32] Today, as I work on this, eleven of fourteen Maldivan cabinet members are convening in the ocean. Our literal footprints (littoral) thanks to coltan (columbium, now niobium, and tantalum), to American Mining Fields lending a leer jet, to outsourcing satellite surveys of the Congo to NASA and its "active extraction phase" replacing "mass scale looting," like signed wetsuits can be auctioned, and bought back, @ protectmaldives.com, to help keep their chain of atolls, delicate barrier reefs. As "greener economies" (gorilla ashtrays) (and only one example) grows increasingly suspicious in step with the polar chance for safeguards protecting against the "unnatural," the desires in the signifier and the audibility of one's actual referent will or won't behave more unclearly. (Standard genesis through apocalypse, a thing is a thing, the zero never was; space's dark matter, 73% of "universal density," frenzied wave borrowed and repaid; particle's antiparticle, "empty" space's "negative pressure" expanding the observable average, where stars come through to the naked eye yet, zero. [45] Human-time-tested logorrheic failure, finally become, at least according to our buzzword chance to understand, and translate, rather *at home,* recognizable *as it* and so, antagonistic.) We'll call this "life, living." Baudrillard alive and well, this place's future is in its way, certain.

"But it's not a diminution of humanness I wish to make, rather a scale for its diverse presence…All that would matter to me, finally, as a writer, is that the scale and the place of our common living be recognized," Creeley writes. [33] If a final resolution to the dilemma is not immediately forthcoming, perhaps the inquirer is wise to cull a workable fiction. After all, to imagine the determinable *health* of environments, so long as most humans occupy them, depends on us—industrious, error-prone, earthen vessels of the nonhuman's production—the question then would be something along the lines of, what is the eco-logical function or value of fictions and their formation? All sites of this produce would be questioned as nodes in local networks and beyond where objective understanding is bound to variable experiences, frictions, conceptions, basic and elaborate exchanges, where each participant understandably changes the event (and vice versa)—the more we may participate in the procreative and documentary understanding of some aspect of a thing, the less we may participate in its other aspects (and so the more and less that thing may have itself participated. Heisenberg's negativity is unexpectedly tender, ecocritical.).

---

[45] There are two main interpretations for this disparity: either the universe began with a small preference for matter (total ███████████ of the universe different from zero), or the universe was originally perfectly symmetric, but somehow a set of phenomena contributed to a small imbalance in favour of matter over time. The second point of view is preferred, although there is no clear experimental evidence &c

In order to engage words and texts in ways that bind the apparent contraries of constructivism and ecocriticism, are other languages required? Do we find writing practices allowing human and nonhuman environments, each paradoxically constituted by the other, undermining and respecting their antagonistic formulations? And what's the point of such fiction?

As I mentioned at the outset, it is my opinion that these questions have been asked before, wherever one can discern from a range of considerations the poet's attention to surroundings and impacts therein. Take the opening "Instead of a Preface" from Anna Akhmatova's "Requiem 1935-1940," published in 1963:

> In the terrible years of the Yezhov terror I spent seventeen months waiting in line outside the prison in Leningrad. One day somebody in the crowd identified me. Standing behind me was a woman, with lips blue from the cold, who had, of course, never heard me called by name before. Now she started out of the torpor common to us all and asked me in a whisper (everyone whispered there):
> "Can you describe this?"
> And I said: "I can."
> Then something like a smile passed fleetingly over what had once been her face. [34]

What concerns me here is the speaker's position and reaction to this position in light of her relation to the blue-lipped woman. The speaker acknowledges the source of her own anonymity while glossing the fact of the woman's; the woman does not know the speaker's name while the opposite passes unmentioned; and this chance for empathy is brought into bluish light. The speaker situates herself in a relation both passive and constructive in light of what understanding can be revealed. She is agent, and she is symptom, and of a common lot awaiting news at the prison wall's drab stone against unmentioned skies in defiance, against the temperateness infecting the body of someone who bears it in like defiance, and each side of proverbial fences occurring much for the sake of something its own. Part of the poetical success of the passage is the illumination of belief in power relations across scale and the prideful provocations (not the least of which, the writing itself) to the frigid and careless brutality of the scene, the most immediately sensory and seemingly indestructible of which is not of human origin.

However. The moment she awakens to the "whisper" from the "torpor common to us all," the moment volition intimates itself, in the form of a question, as the chance to "describe this," the occasion is the *actual possibility* of each stranger's respite from more common realities. In the midst of their shared absence, housed in stone facades, a cold void, the "smile passed fleetingly" across the blued lips of the inquirer, waiting for news, is, in all its ephemerality, a mock and jeer of impossible recovery, power and bliss aimed everywhere. This re-called, recordable proof of the environmental value of humanitarian imaginations gives an ethic "instead of a preface"—once recognizable by name, the poet is recognizable as a service to people *as* a service to places, shaper of *memory*—low flame to circulation.

I have not lost sight of identifying a practice in conversation with the nonhuman. Though Akhmatova's "Requiem" is concerned with distinctly human things, the concern for *accurate description of an actual place* ("this") suggests something less concerned *for* itself than with *knowledge of* itself. In this regard, the passage shows a poetic tuned to the need for inventiveness, otherwise the mercy of surroundings. The approach is not escapist, nor imperial. Akhmatova gives the listener *a* place that was and was not *the* place, and much that is important is left the better for it. Were this passage written today, it would satisfy Tarlo's injunction "to get beyond the obsession with linguistic experimentation *per se,* to transcend readings [and therefore, writings] in which form is fetishised above the intertexts, ideology, politics and contexts with which the work engages." [35] Tarlo is interested in the ecocritical possibilities of "linguistically innovative" poetry":

> In fact, suspicion of the referential element of language in LIP is deeply desirable for the poet concerned with nature and environment. When I turned to the poetry itself, rather than its criticisms, I found that it was that very sense of the gap between our language and our world that preserves respect for the non-linguistic world in these writers. [36]

For Tarlo, "the post-structuralist approach is no longer the only filter through which to view the avant-garde," [37] so that a "linguistically innovative" constructivist orientation might embrace an ecocritical insistence on faithfully rendering Levin's "autonomous nature."

A selection from Charles Olson's *Maximus Poems* serves as a case in point:

> by the way into the woods
>
> Indian   otter   orient
> "Lake"   ponds
>
> show me   (exhibit
> myself) [38]

Elsewhere the poet privileges pre-cognitive sense perception: "Sensibility within the organism by movement of its own tissues…Wash the ego out, in its own bath." [39] If syntax is "the very form of thought," [40] Olson seeks what is beyond that form, what surrounds it—a pool of visceral data, the raw material of thinking. In this poem a field of signifiers that *want* to obey syntactic rule effects a subject. In a sense, the field has narrative agency. For example, following on the left-to-right heels of the awkwardly normal phrasal construction "show me," parenthetical "exhibit" arrives first as an injunction to something, verb; but the spacing that isolates it are syntactic ruptures in which the speaker's parenthetical "myself" arrives also as "the exhibit"; "exhibit" *finally* oscillates between verb and noun. As this *potential* of language is *released*, perceived entities—nouns—"show" the speaker, or the speaker is imploring them to. The visual field is being allowed to do its own work, or the poet is asking it to, opening the floodgates of its medium(s).

But how do we receive this potential given to words? Does it reflect any "nature?" Does the vision of the nonhuman vis-à-vis the speaker reflect the place's actual conditions, or the reader's need for something legible? What are words and what are they for? There's more than a hint of religious bliss here, so that Kathleen Matthews's take on *Paterson* is useful. In it, Williams "creates a local anthropomorphic deity of rock and water and also uses the sound of water over rock as the major metaphor for a living language." [41] Instead of "the sound of water over rock," Olson (here) prefers fleshy-mammal-bobbing-in-still-lake and its meditative silence. Language is medium in this place, charged interface between things through which the speaker's self-awareness, facing what he very much is not, is predicated. His English channels its material participants into vessels of historical significance, like capitalized "Indian 'Lake'" to "orient" the poem within its human trajectory, whose bare infinitive still otherwise provokes; stripped of its definite rule (as denotative source) ("otter orient?"), this novel, perhaps younger English prolongs the attention to *finding* inside of and beyond translatable, sharable, root-bound chronicles ("ponds," plural) (field, project, becoming). "By way of the poem itself to, all the way over to, the reader," [42] the difficulty attending problem syntax also spotlights the felicitous, abstract, personal nature of the poem's signified psychological terrain, a gesture, given the plausibility of its place, to illuminate yet mock everything else that would be about it, finding non-definitive spaces *readers must enter.* As if, standing there, behind its speaker, receiving, acting, participating with their encounter(s)—old and new, who or what did the writing?

With little to guide us beyond recourse to absent syntax (by way of its problematized *presence*), the "reader" (speaker) draws from beyond familiar "grammar" (place) (expands contracting, dwells and evolves, devolving) in order to uncover what *other* voices commune, as if *that* is somehow where *each* could have been more fully. Even if *he* won't exactly, the field invites us to look for ourselves—how we become it, *that, ours.* The "way into the woods," or (possess) such passage, every direction, kinesthesia, tasting, articulating, whether one's self or to a page, moving (imp)ersonal way—take or abstract and involve the familiar in order to scribble in the shared site which, in order to be true, would respect the distance from what lay beyond itself attempting to be one's own little blooming and rooted dependence. Resistance to closure means we bring something useful into these "woods"—ironic figure suggesting the usual or unusual end be shady adventure, trial, more careful footfalls. "(exhibit / myself)": On this dirt path, half in the shadow of smaller leaves, the perceiving "I" and its *sources outwardly drawn, to be displayed.*

Through literature, can one "transcend the restrictions of signifier and image?" [43] Via words, can the city's inhabitant step beyond his virtual life to experience an "ecosublime" whose aftermath is the transformed self, "grounded to the ecological referent…the recognition that we aren't so isolated after all?" [44] I wish to suggest that an ecopoetic sensitive to constructivist dilemmas, one that recognizes that "it is the pleasure and authority of writing that it invents a life to live in the first place," [45] is an old concern whose gloss distances one from the ethical, honest and accurate dimensions of ecocritical production. That it benefits from indulging the antagonisms and contraries of our "heteroglot opinion"—of that subject and object, true and false, idea and thing—insofar as this could help undermine fraught involvements in the material places in which we are.

Embracing (perhaps) inescapable complicity, perhaps forms of care appears to temper approaches to vulnerable things.

Notes

1. Lawrence Buell, quoted in "Forum on Literatures of the Environment," *PMLA* 114.5 (1999): 1091.
2. Jonathan Levin, "Review: Beyond Nature? Recent Work in Ecocriticism," *Contemporary Literature* 43.1 (2002): 175.
3. Sarah Blair, "Cultural Geography and the Place of the Literary," *American Literary History* 10.3 (1998): 551.
4. Levin, 176.
5. Ibid., 177.
6. Ibid., 178.
7. Maurice Merleau-Ponty, *The Visible and the Invisible* (Evanston, IL: Northwestern UP, 1968), 171-9.
8. Levin, 178.
9. Ibid., quoting Leonard Scigaj.
10. Sara Blair, "Cultural Geography and the Place of the Literary," *American Literary History* 10.3 (1998): 551.
11. Harriet Tarlo, "Radical Landscapes: experiment and environment in contemporary poetry," *Jacket* 32 (April 2007): paragraph 4.
12. Mikhail Bakhtin, "Discourse in the Novel," in *Literary Theory: An Anthology* (Malden, MA: Blackwell, 1998), 32.
13. Ibid., 35.
14. Ibid.
15. Ibid., 32-44.
16. Jacques Derrida, "Différance," in *Literary Theory: An Anthology* (Malden, MA: Blackwell, 1998), 392, italics mine.
17. Ibid., 399-400.
18. Ibid., 396.
19. Ibid., 387.
20. Ibid.
21. Ibid., 402.
22. Jean Baudrillard, *Jean Baudrillard: Selected Writings* (Stanford: Stanford UP, 1988), 166.
23. Michael Cohen, quoted in "Forum on Literatures of the Environment," *PMLA* 114.5 (1999): 1092.
24. For example, Scott McLean, "Shaking the Pumpkin, Shaking the Word: A Poet's Plea," *Pacific Coast Philology* 34.2 (1999): 149-50.

25. Blair, 544.

26. Ibid., 545-7.

27. Ibid., 552.

28. Ibid., 556.

29. Ibid., 547.

30. Ibid., quoting Wayne Franklin and Michael Steiner, 551-2.

31. Ibid., quoting Franklin and Steiner, John Graves, and Nancy Duncan, 551.

32. Ibid., quoting Edward Ayers, Patricia Nelson Limerick, Stephen Nissenbaum, and Peter S. Onuf, 552.

33. Robert Creeley, *Autobiography* (New York: Hanuman Books, 1990), 54-5.

34. Anna Akhmatova, *Poems of Akhmatova* (New York: Mariner, 1973), 99.

35. Tarlo, paragraph 4.

36. Ibid.

37. Ibid.

38. Charles Olson, *Maximus Poems* (Berkeley: U of California Press, 1983), 203.

39. Ibid., *Selected Writings* (New York: New Directions, 1966), 181.

40. Charles O. Hartman, *Free Verse: An Essay on Prosody* (Evanston, IL: Northwestern UP, 1980), quoting Harvey Gross, 128.

41. Lee Rozelle, "Ecocritical City: Modernist Reactions to Urban Environments in 'Miss Lonelyhearts' and 'Paterson,'" *Twentieth Century Literature* 48.1 (2002), quoting Kathleen Matthews, 113.

42. Olson, *Selected Writings,* 16.

43. Rozelle, 114.

44. Ibid.

45. Creeley, 10.

Bibliography [46]

Akhmatova, Anna. *Poems of Akhmatova.* Translated by Stanley Kunitz and Max Hayward. New York: Mariner, 1973.

"Forum on Literatures of the Environment." *PMLA* 114.5 (1999): 1089-1104.

Bakhtin, Mikhail. "Discourse in the Novel." In *Literary Theory: An Anthology,* edited by Julie Rivkin and Michael Ryan. Revised Edition. Malden, MA: Blackwell, 1998. 32-44.

Baudrillard, Jean. *Jean Baudrillard: Selected Writings.* Edited by Mark Poster. Stanford: Stanford UP, 1988.

Blair, Sara. "Cultural Geography and the Place of the Literary." *American Literary History* 10.3 (1998): 544-67.

Creeley, Robert. *Autobiography.* New York: Hanuman Books, 1990.

Derrida, Jacques. "Différance." In *Literary Theory: An Anthology.* Edited by Julie Rivkin and Michael Ryan. Revised Edition. Malden, MA: Blackwell, 1998. 385-407.

Hartman, Charles O. *Free Verse: An Essay on Prosody.* Evanston, IL: Northwestern UP, 1980.

Levin, Jonathan. "Review: Beyond Nature? Recent Work in Ecocriticism." *Contemporary Literature* 43.1 (2002): 171-86.

McLean, Scott. "Shaking the Pumpkin, Shaking the Word: A Poet's Plea." *Pacific Coast Philology* 34.2 (1999): 149-62.

---

[46] Karen Armstrong Alessandro Barbero Battleground the film and UMass Amherst ROTC Minuteman Battalion Dan Beachy-Quick Ed Bernays the Buddha Jay S Bybee Dan Chiasson the CLMP Code of Ethics Dante D H Lawrence Anita Diamant Raymond Federman John T Flynn Philippe Galle via Maarten van Heemskerck Kenneth Goldsmith via Kent Johnson Roger S Gottlieb Diogenes and Phidias and the Greek Ruth Hill Susan Howe Ann Hutchinson küçük İskender (little Alexander) and Nâzim Hikmet via Murat Nemet-Nejat David Kaufmann Kiva ads via Hulu Abdellatif Laâbi via Gordon Hadfield and Nancy Hadfield Dorothy Lee Heller Levinson Linda Pastan Diane di Prima Myung Mi Kim 1996 Mollie McDonough Karl Marx Nabokov the NAPT Poetry Therapy Code of Ethics The New York Times the OED Charles Olson Research Planning Inc The Gulf War Oil Spill Twelve Years Later the Consequences of Ecoterrorism those habitats exposed to the greatest amount of wave activity contain the smallest amount of residual oil Chuck Richardson John Ruskin Jared Schickling's thesis Jim Sheeler Richard Slotkin David Archer and Alex Cameron via SOCIA Ltd Academy for Justice Commissioning the Challenges of Collaborative Leadership Wallace Stevens John Cleves Symmes Junior Jean Toomer USPTO Electronic Filing System Joseph Warton Simone Weil Walt Whitman one enormous wiki W C Williams Dorothy Wordsworth William Elizabeth Wurtzel John Yoo

Merleau-Ponty, Maurice. *The Visible and the Invisible.* Evanston, IL: Northwestern UP, 1968.

Olson, Charles. *Maximus Poems.* Berkeley: U of California Press, 1983.

- - - . *Selected Writings.* Edited by Robert Creeley. New York: New Directions, 1966.

Rozelle, Lee. "Ecocritical City: Modernist Reactions to Urban Environments in 'Miss Lonelyhearts' and 'Paterson.'" *Twentieth Century Literature* 48.1 (2002): 100-115.

Tarlo, Harriet. "Radical Landscapes: experiment and environment in contemporary poetry." *Jacket* 32 (April 2007): http://jacketmagazine.com/32/p-tarlo.shtml.

OR

What most immediately comes to mind when thinking of " ▮▮▮▮▮▮▮▮▮▮▮▮ "
are its ▮▮▮▮▮ dimensions, whose attitude toward poetry is that it should be conscious
of the ways in which it engages the real, actual world it inhabits. Fair enough. But one is
inclined to finding a doubleness in the ways of it—always other than they seem, always
other than how they, on the one hand, actually are. And more concretely than this, the
work happens by way of the frictional transfers or exchanges of two or more other things.
It is agent and production, cause and symptom, all at once. "Birthed" is the ▮▮▮▮-laden
term, yet seems to point at an inhuman, universally operative principle—all kinds of
symptomatic things will be "born" of the human organism bearing its Y chromosome.
This is thin terrain, as the work will risk making light of ▮▮▮▮▮ concerns, or certain
actual things in a people's lives to which the author has no access, something it does not
want to do.

It navigates this risk by establishing the public life of the work. For example, it sees that
a culture of identity politics, political correctness, emasculated heroics, in the age of
▮▮▮▮▮▮▮ all help promote an ▮▮▮▮▮▮ individualism whose "dim-brained brutality
thwarts its own purposes."

Thus the pronomial life of its manuscripts could be queered, if they are to be tender,
supple, remove veils, the poetry is at times brutal and cold. In its pursuit of inhuman
things that apply to people and their larger lives, its author mines its own shortcomings
before suggesting more general failures. In this way, that the hand is one of its most
sensitive intrigues, the text is its route to some community.

Which necessitates one eye to two coaxes, "she" and "he," embedded particularly,
pioneers, a historical place. The work finds in them national psyches antagonizing their

Made in the USA
Monee, IL
07 July 2026

56551627R00070